Savour of Scotland /a Scottish diversity

Spectator Publications Limited

Devised and produced by
Spectator Publications Limited © 1975
Treatment by Lindley Abbatt
Edited by David Fisher
Photography (unless otherwise credited) by
Michael Cyprien
Typesetting and litho-origination by
Tinling (1973) Limited
Text paper Hi-Speed Blade 115 g/m²
Supplied by Wiggins Teape Limited
from their Waterton Mills,
Bucksburn, near Aberdeen
Printed and bound by
Tinling (1973) Limited,

ISBN 900869 25 9

CONTENTS

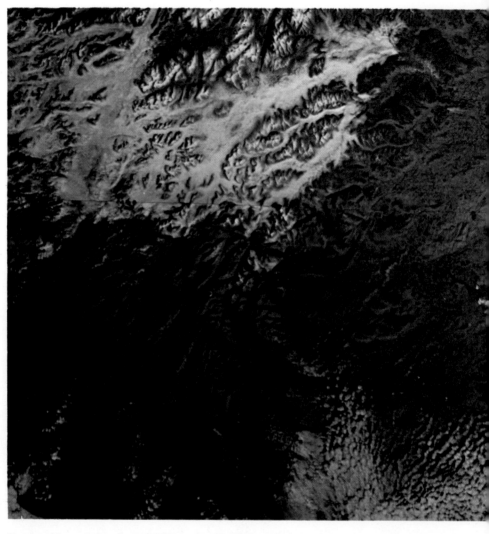

Scotland is an Atlantic end of Europe. To this position it owes much of its unrivalled scenery, its boisterous climate and weather, its ecology and geography. Although Scotland has only half the area of England and Wales, its deeply indented coastline is twice as long as theirs together and is fringed by over 180 islands. The surrounding seas are only 25 miles apart between the rivers Clyde and Forth. Maritime influences penetrate everywhere. Scotland is a very old land, the ages of her rocks spanning the greater part of known geological time. Millions of years of ice, sea and weather erosion have created highly varied country, which has been further modified during the past few thousand years by man. Large parts still remain sparsely inhabited, in contrast to the core where over two-thirds of Scots now live.

The shape of Scotland has probably endured in broad outline for around ten million years. Originally a high plateau, it has gradually had its overall height reduced and its

The Face of Scotland / Dr. Margaret C. Storrie

surface broken up, so that it consists today of three major topographic divisions. The Highlands and Islands are the most mountainous part of Britain. Many peaks rise to over 3000 feet, and Ben Nevis (4406 feet) is the highest in Europe west of the Vosges and the Massif Central. Even in the Central Lowlands volcanic outpourings have produced plateaus reaching to over 2000 feet. South east of a line from Girvan to Dunbar lie the Southern Uplands, where the highest peak is the picturesque Tinto (2335 feet).

One of the most striking results of the different rates at which harder and softer rocks have been eroded has been the marked graining of the landscape. Many of Scotland's landforms trend from south west to north east, as in the Great Glen, the Minch and Outer Hebrides, the Central Lowlands and Inner Hebrides, and the Southern Uplands. Scotland's multiplicity of islands is also partly due to this 'differential erosion', as well as to changes in the level of the sea.

There is also a striking relationship in many areas of the country between rock type and scenery, a correspondence that affects both the altitude and the form of the ground. Some of the most spectacular scenery occurs near the north western extremity. There, vast thicknesses of sandstones end in great stepped buttresses and cliffs, as in Stac Polly and Suilven. Granite masses form the rounded summits of the Cairngorms, and the floor of Rannoch Moor. The junction of the Highlands with the Lowlands is emphasised by a belt of grit which stands out as a line of 3000-foot hills that includes Ben Lomond. Elsewhere, quartzite forms the glistening Paps of Jura, while limestone outcrops invariably show up amidst luxurious green pastures, in parts of Shetland, Durness, Lismore and the Isle of Islay. Volcanic rocks form the highest barren parts of Ben Nevis and of the Three Sisters of Glencoe, while the lavas of Mull, Skye and Eigg are horizontally stepped with cliffs and scarps; the vertically jointed columns of Fingal's Cave on Staffa are probably even better known. In the Central Lowlands, the connection between hills and volcanic activity is very close. Volcanic plugs (the cores of former volcanoes) are notable, like Dumbarton Rock, a fortress since pre-Roman times. In the Southern Uplands fairly thin layers of rocks have weathered to form smooth, rounded hills. Many sedimentary rocks throughout Scotland give subdued contours, although there are exceptions like the red sandstone of Hoy in Orkney, which forms cliffs some 1100 feet above the wild sea, with a 450-foot stack nearby.

With its great geological variety, Scotland has become one of the classical study areas of the world. Edinburgh, for example, became a leading centre of geology and other earth sciences during the late eighteenth century Scottish Renaissance. More 'recent' changes (of the last 5000 to 10,000 years) are easily visible, such as the glacially deepened lochs (the Loch Ness Monster may live as much as 750 feet below the surface!) and glens of the west; the 'tail' deposits behind the crags on which fortifications like the Edinburgh and Stirling castles stand; the many raised beaches and old shorelines with their sea caves, used formerly by smugglers.

The glens of the Western Highlands are usually much shorter and steeper-sided than are the eastern straths, with their wide valleys and broad rivers. In the west, most of the glens were already valleys before the ice came, and the subsequent drowning of their mouths by sea-level changes has produced the long coastline of magnificent fiords and lochs. During World War II access to these sea lochs could be controlled by means of booms, so they became important convoy-gathering bases (e.g. the Clyde). Their depth made them useful for submarine manoeuvres and torpedo testing (Gare Loch and Loch Long), and they are now much in demand for launching or constructing the massive structures used by the North Sea oil industry, and for supertanker terminals.

Above sea-level, the steep-sided western glens have been exploited for hydro-electricity production. Water falls rapidly through penstocks down the sides of the valley to drive turbines at the bottom. The Loch Awe pumped storage scheme re-cycles water, so as to eliminate the need for large-scale damming. In the Central Lowlands, the large firths are also the drowned estuaries of preglacial rivers. They have through history presented communications problems, that were solved by ferries until railway bridges were built across the Forth and Tay in the early twentieth century. New road bridges across the Clyde, Forth and Tay have been constructed during the last decade.

Scotland's rich geological base was important to the industrial revolution, especially rocks of the carboniferous series. Though worked out in many areas, coal is still being mined under the Firth of Forth. The presence of ironstone led to the establishment of much of Scotland's heavy industry, and it is often claimed that the world's oil industry began in the oil shales of West Lothian. Gold from Leadhills was used in the sixteenth century to make the Scottish regalia, and there was even a 'gold rush' to the Strath of Kildonan (Sutherland) in the 1860s, that involved some 400 miners. Silver, lead, zinc and copper have all been mined superficially (and wastefully) and the element strontium takes its name from the discovery of strontianite in 1791 at Strontian in Ardnamurchan (Argyll). A very pure cretacious sandstone some 110 feet thick at Loch Aline in Morven (Argyll) is much sought after for glass making. Scotland's dwindling mineral stocks are at present being re-evaluated, particularly in the Highlands and Islands, though prospects do not seem particularly hopeful.

There are some important deficiencies in Scotland's resources, quite apart from worked-out coal seams. In the past most Scottish buildings, large and small, public and private, were built of stone, honey-coloured or red sandstones being the most popular. As the use of bricks superseded that of dressed stone, Scotland found herself deficient in good brick-making materials. Rather poor quality bricks can be made from carboniferous clays, but for weatherproofing and aesthetic reasons they require facing. This is often achieved by 'harling', a form of pebbledash. An alternative building technique has, since 1945, become a Scottish hallmark: no-fines concrete. This is a mix of readily-available loose aggregate bound with cement in a proportion of about 8 or 10:1, poured into shutters, set and then covered, often with harling.

For long the seas around the Scottish coasts were regarded chiefly as ship carriers and producers of organic life. Both functions are still important, with centralised modern facilities. Most parts of the coast have a fairly large tidal range, usually measured in double figures of feet. This helps the growth of seaweed, gathered in the past for kelping (making soda for use in glass and soap manufacture). Even today, there is still a sizable alginate industry in Scotland, producing compounds for cosmetics, foodstuffs and other uses. On the negative side, the tides made necessary the construction of docks and other engineering works in the upper estuaries.

It is only in the last decade that Scotland's continental shelf has been shown to have considerable deposits of gas and oil. Two vast areas of sedimentation to the east and west of Scotland come together north of the Shetlands. East is the North Sea Basin: shallow in the south but reaching 600 feet in depth off Shetland. To the west the continental shelf is part of the so-called 'Atlantic Province'. Exploration for oil and gas is beginning in the Hebridean part of the shelf.

The relationship between the oil industry and the Scottish coast is dominated by two themes. One is distance: that between the oilfields and the shore is considerable: even helicopter trips from Aberdeen to the farthest oil rigs take several hours, but supply ships from Dundee or Peterhead take much longer. The length of the pipeline from the Forties field to Cruden Bay, near Peterhead, completed in October 1974, is more than a hundred and ten miles. The other main theme is the impact on the coastal areas of back-up activities. Along several stretches of coast, land is rapidly being reclaimed from the sea to make new flat sites for large constructions (e.g. Nigg Bay on Moray Firth and Ardyne Point, Argyll), or for service terminals (e.g. Peterhead and Montrose). (In the more remote areas, where the influx of men and equipment (albeit perhaps only for a relatively short construction phase) may seriously disrupt the local society, the justification for the activity is questionable. Expanding this land-based technology to support and service drilling rigs in northern waters over 600 feet, for oil many thousands of feet below the seabed, is a formidable technological challenge. Advantages and disadvantages for Scotland as a country and as a people are precariously balanced, with many political reverberations.

Many other activities besides the oil industry are affected by Scottish climate and weather. Latitude—from 54°30 in the Mull of Galloway to almost 60°N. at Muckle Flugga in the Shetlands—has been the major factor, with altitude also being of great importance. In a relatively small country, the variety in both space and time is as apparent in Scottish weather as it is in other Scottish characteristics. Daffodils run wild in Galloway by March, but the Shetland crop does not bloom until May or June. There are similar contrasts between east and west: many of the Hebrides rarely see snow, whereas it may lie for weeks in the Central Highlands, and on Ben Nevis for over 200 days of the year.

But the most notable characteristic of the climate and weather is the omnipresent wind. Current housing standards are higher in Scotland than further south, though modern materials replace the thick stone walls of bygone days. Clothing tends to be thicker and warmer. Shelter becomes an important factor, whether in the form of trees for farm animals and wild life, or covered shopping centres (like that at Cumbernauld New Town) for the twentieth century family. Winds are most apparent on the islands, the sea coasts, and at higher altitudes: climbing accidents are often due to wind exposure in near-Arctic conditions. Because of them, the treeline in the west is very low, whereas in the east it may struggle up to about 2000 feet.

Edinburgh, after all, is nearer to the Arctic than to the Mediterranean, but its

soubriquet 'Athens of the North' refers to its architecture rather than to its climate. Yet, thanks to the oceans around it, Scotland's climate is much warmer in winter than might be expected from its latitude, even if cooler in summer. The most frequent weather systems come from the North Atlantic, usually bringing the 'showers and bright periods' so familiar in the daily weather forecast. Once again, regional differences in weather are important. At times in Edinburgh the road surface of the Mound may have its electric underblanket switched on to melt the ice while the Hebrides may be basking in mild winter sunshime. By contrast, eastern Scotland may in summer suffer mists or 'haars', when air from the continent becomes chilled as it crosses the North Sea; simultaneously in the west, or in the Spey valley, temperatures may be over 25° under clear skies.
The driest months of the year tend to be from February to April, with a good chance also in September, when colours in the landscape are at their most magnificent. The wettest months are from October to December—and also August, the prime holiday month.

Man's use of the land in Scotland is governed partly by the natural environment, but also by society and economy. Characteristic of Scottish land resources is the marked imbalance between good and poor agricultural land: really good farm land is rare and randomly distributed. Much crop tillage is concentrated in the east, where barley is now the most important crop, for brewing, distilling and for fattening famous beef breeds. Oats and some winter wheat are also grown, but less than 20% of the cropland is under roots or potatoes. Grasslands, rotation and permanent, are one of Scotland's most valuable resources, forming the basis of a world-renowned dairy industry originally

based on Ayrshires. Golf courses are perhaps equally well-known consumers of Scottish grass.

Much of the area of Scotland, however, is occupied by land that is not under cultivation: 'rough grazing' (some of it very rough indeed) occupies almost two-thirds of the total area, providing the staple feed for hill cattle, sheep, deer and red grouse. The old black Highland cattle have been replaced by improved breeds: West Highland, Galloway and Luing, but all require some supplementary feed. Blackface and Cheviot sheep thrive on heather-covered moorland, when it is well managed. Heather is evergreen and a year-long source of fodder. Its management was widely practised for sheep, before grouse made it fashionable and thereby profitable in Victorian times. Grouse stocks feed on young heather and shelter under older heather; in the wetter west they need several times the area per brace than in the east where heather grows better. Grouse do not mix as well as sheep or cattle do with people, so they inhibit the multiple use of the land. Deer provides more competition for rough grazing, especially in the west: so much so that the present population of about 200,000 has to be controlled under the Red Deer Commission's culling programme.

Peatlands are another of the more obvious features of the landscape; they cover about one-sixth of the total area, and extend over one-third of the surface of Sutherland and two-thirds of that of Caithness. Blanket-bog, the most common type, began accumulating about 7,500 years ago, and is now tens of feet thick in places. Roman legionaries guarding the Antonine Wall to keep out the Picts probably cut peat to keep out Scottish cold. Ever since, it has been cut for both domestic and industrial uses, but it has certainly never been a cheap fuel in terms of effort or of time. The possibilities of using peat (as in Ireland) as a power station fuel were explored in Caithness, but were abandoned in 1960 and now seem irrelevant with the advent of North Sea oil and gas.

Although only a handful of whisky distilleries continue to use peat as a fuel, the smoke from smouldering peat is still a vital part of the process of making malt from sprouted barley for use in both brewing and distilling. The various organic compounds in the peat play a quintessential part in producing the unique flavour and bouquet of the whisky from each individual distillery. Conversion of some peatlands (especially in the Isle of Lewis in the Outer Hebrides) to grassland have been fairly successful, by draining, application of surface fertiliser and reseeding, but the largest single user of Scotland's peatlands is the Forestry Commission.

Scotland's woodland area still only amounts to about 8.5% of the total land, despite much recent afforestation and reafforestation. This proportion is much higher than in the rest of Great Britain, but is low by most European standards. Scotland is part of the coniferous forest zone of northern Europe, and her present relative treelessness does not reflect the natural vegetation climax in most parts of the country. Despite the wind, large areas are eminently suited for tree growth, as can be seen from the fast growth of many introduced species. Forestry in Scotland directly employs about one in six of a dwindling rural population. The Forestry Commission is Scotland's largest single landowner, private woodlands being only about half as extensive as Commission plantations. The traditional antagonism and competition for land between agriculture and forest is now replaced by enlightened cooperation, and other multiple uses are being accommodated. Of the seven National Forest Parks in Britain, four are in Scotland: Glenmore, Queen Elizabeth, Argyll and Glen Trool, all with good facilities for visitors.

Many of the plantations established by private owners and the Forestry Commission, of Sitka spruce, Scots pine and other species, are now producing thinnings and other commercially-usable timber. Sawmills take some of the output for general purposes, and the bulk market for paper and board manufacture is expanding, although the United Kingdom is still dependent on imported pulp for about 90% of its requirements.

Progress towards a Scottish pulp industry began in the 1950s, culminating in the 1966 opening of the £15 million Wiggins Teape integrated pulp and paper mill at Annat Point in the shadow of Ben Nevis. Scottish forests now provide the bulk of the mill's raw material. In terms of sheer quantity, they could provide it all, but some imported timber needs to be added to the domestic supply to make certain kinds of paper. The site at Annat had several advantages: power and water from the British Aluminium hydro-electric scheme at Fort William; tidal water facilities for imports, and assistance from the Government in housebuilding, improved roads, and a guarantee of rail access continuance. The high grade papers produced by the plant are shipped by rail to southern markets.

The social effects of the mill have been considerable, to say nothing of its part in establishing a renewable resource in the Highlands. It has become a recognised growth point in the West Highlands, stabilising population in a region that was tending to depopulate. At present between 1000 and 1100 are employed directly in the Annat complex, with 2000 or so in the forests, and others providing services. Including family numbers, the multiplier is probably of the order of 7 or 8. One test of the success of the community will come with the new generation of Annat adults who are now beginning to come on the the employment market: will they migrate elsewhere, or will they find the Fort William area one in which they wish to remain?

Emphasis in this chapter has been on the face of Scotland, and on how its natural resources have been utilised and modified by its people. It is at once one of the wildest and one of the most agricultural parts of the United Kingdom. It is also one of the most scenic, with a tourist industry that compares in value to exports of whisky. Most of Scotland's population, however, is an urban one, whether in the Central Lowlands (three million or more), or in other cities, large and small burghs, or villages. For them the land has much to offer for leisure and recreation as well as for employment. Scotland's fresh air, clean and abundant water, magnificent coastal and mountain scenery, afford many and varied recreation opportunities. It is becoming increasingly necessary to reconcile the conservation of natural resources with their economic utilisation and with recreational demands. Many uses of the land and water are compatible with each other, but others are not. Even recreation, if too concentrated on a few attractive but vulnerable areas, may lead to deterioration of amenities in an area like Highland Scotland that exists on a climatic and vegetational margin. Just as geology, grouse and other factors generated research in the past, so the need to plan the multiple use of the Scottish landscape is generating research, sponsored by the Countryside Commission for Scotland, the Scottish Tourist Board, the Highlands and Islands Development Board, and others concerned with maintaining the unique appearance of the face of Scotland.

Chronicles of the Past/Joan Rees

For most people, even including many Scots, the history of Scotland is blurred and confused, like the mist over the mountains, swirling away now and again to reveal certain bold individual heroes and vivid passages of drama. In a small compass, little more can be done than to outline a few broad historical divisions, and to set in perspective against them some of the more familiar figures.

Throughout the centuries, Scottish history has been influenced by the natural difficulties of the terrain. The coastline is rugged and full of inlets, surrounded by a scatter of lonely islands; the country is divided within itself by the great barrier of the Highlands, and from neighbouring England by the lovely but bleak lands of the Borders; much of the country is agriculturally unproductive. By its very nature, Scotland was always difficult to unify, and until comparatively recent times it represented to outsiders an alien country, wild, remote and mysterious.

Even to the historians, the picture of the earliest days is vague and puzzling. By the time the Romans arrived in Britain, Scotland seems to have been occupied for some three thousand years. The first stone age settlements were in the Oban Caves and the Hebrides, and among the most fascinating of the ancient sites are the well preserved Skara Brae settlement on the West Mainland of Orkney, and the Megalithic monument of Maes Howe in Stenness. Other waves of invaders followed: Bronze age men who worked ornaments from the gold obtained from Ireland; in about the 10th century B.C. the first recognised Celtic stock whose language formed the basis of Gaelic; and in the 4th century, a group of Celts from whose language were developed Breton, Welsh, and Cornish, among whom were the Picts. The circular towers known as the brochs were thought to have been built by the Picts, and hundreds of these once stood in the north and west of Scotland and on some of the Islands.

The Romans never succeeded in conquering Scotland, although the famous general Julius Agricola reached as far North as Stirling. They found a wild mountainous country of thick forests and undrained swamps abounding in wild animals and providing the perfect setting for what we know now as guerilla warfare. Later legend described it as "a land where the air was so poisonous that no human being or creature other than serpents could survive there more than half an hour"—perhaps the first reference to the Loch Ness monster.

Finally, the Romans retreated and tried to pen up the unruly inhabitants behind two walls, the wall of Hadrian and further North the wall of Antoninus, thus depriving Scotland of the good roads and well regulated civic and commercial life that were established in the South. A lasting benefit left by the invaders was the new religion of Christianity, spread in Scotland by the great missionary saints Ninian and Columba. It has been suggested that the Romans introduced the bagpipes, a theory that anyone who has heard the plaintive pipes of the Abruzzi shepherds will be inclined to believe.

By this time, other waves of immigrants had come in: the Scots from Ireland, soon to be followed by the Angles, Saxons, and early Norse invaders. After many years of unrest, in 843, the Picts were finally united with the Scots under Kenneth MacAlpin, who became the first King of Alba—the land of the Scots.

Kenneth was crowned at his Perthshire capital of Forteviot, using the Stone of Destiny from the Pictish capital of Scone, which later became the traditional coronation place of Scottish kings. The Stone was supposed to have been originally the pillow on which Jacob dreamed his famous dream, and subsequently the Coronation Stone of the Irish kings at Tara. A less romantic view finds it bears a marked resemblance to the sandstone in the region of Scone. But whatever its origin, its mystic significance has persisted into the 20th century.

Kenneth reigned for sixteen turbulent years, and his successors reaped an uneasy inheritance. They had two major difficulties: the constant waves of Viking invaders, who founded Norse settlements on the mainland and became virtually the rulers of the islands; and the Tanist rule of succession, which meant that every King had a "Tanist" or heir apparent, usually a brother or cousin, recognised at the time of his own succession. In other words, until this was superseded by the feudal rule of inheritance by the eldest surviving son after the reign of Malcolm III, dangerous rivalry was a built-in feature of the system.

The best known example of the defects of Tanistry was the murder of Duncan by Macbeth. Shakespeare based his magnificent study of ambition, murder, and guilt on the account given in the *Chronicles* of Holinshed. Shakespeare took liberties with Holinshed, and Holinshed had already taken liberties with history. In fact, far from a venerable old figure, Duncan was the grandson of the powerful ruler Malcolm II, who had selected him to succeed, even though the older Macbeth had at least an equal claim. After six not very successful years' rule, Duncan was killed by Macbeth, either as tradition has it at his castle at Cawdor, or perhaps in the heat of battle.

Duncan's two sons escaped to safety, Malcolm to be brought up in Northumbria, and Donald Bane, who was to follow his brother as Scotland's last truly Celtic king, in the Hebrides. But perhaps Shakespeare was right about Macbeth's sense of guilt, for in 1050 he seems to have gone on a pilgrimage to Rome. His wife, Gruoch, was also of royal stock, and was a significant woman, if not quite the power behind the throne that Shakespeare represented. The end came in 1057, when Macbeth was defeated and killed by Duncan's son Malcolm, with the help of his uncle, Siward, Earl of Northumbria.

Malcolm III was known as Malcolm Canmore, or Bighead, presumably a description of his physical appearance, not his personality. He reigned for thirty five years, marrying first Inigbiord, widow of the Norse Earl of the Orkneys, and, after her death, the saintly Margaret, the educated, pious, and influential sister of Edgar Atheling who, but for William the Conqueror, might have been the English King. During his long reign, Malcolm III was at odds with the Norman rulers of England, invading five times in an attempt to extend his dominion into Northumbria. In his last attack, he and his eldest son by Margaret were both killed at Alnwick.

Perhaps because of his English wife, Malcolm Canmore begun supplanting the ancient Gaelic tongue by English, and he had introduced surnames; two factors which contributed to the separation of the Highlanders from the rest of the country, and to the emergence of the Clans. It is not difficult to imagine how the fierce loyalties of the Clans were fostered in the remote areas of the mountains and glens, bound together by the ties of blood, tradition, language, place, by the need for protection, and by the great names that are now so familiar.

The period from 1124 until 1371 begins with the reign of David I and ends with the reign of David II.

The ninth son of Malcolm III, David I came from the court of Henry I in England to take up his inheritance. A man of charm and education, with a wealthy Norman wife, David I carried on the policies initiated by Malcolm Canmore by introducing many features of the society he had observed in England. This move towards feudalism and the rule of law was not always popular, particularly with the Clans. He played an important part in bringing the old Celtic Christianity into line with the other branches of the Catholic church, dividing the country into dioceses with a system of parishes under Anglo-Norman bishops.

The commercial life of the country was stimulated by the establishment of the Royal Burghs—Dunfermline, Berwick, Roxburgh, Edinburgh, Perth, Sterling, and Aberdeen—with the right to hold fairs, trading monopolies in such essential commodities as bread, beer, and cloth, and freedom from tolls. For the first time, metal currency was issued from the two Royal mints at Berwick and Roxburgh.

David's thirty years of progressive rule were in the main peaceful, but in the perennial Scottish hope of annexing Northumbria, he became involved in the war of succession in England which followed the death of Henry I, and was defeated at the famous Battle of the Standard, so called because of the high cross and banners of the saints raised on one of the English waggons.

It was David's grandson, known as William the Lion, who in 1165 was the first Scottish King to enter into an alliance with France against England, which renewed through many centuries became known as the Auld Alliance, and meant that the two countries undertook to maintain a united front against England. It would be difficult to argue whether the alliance was always of benefit to the Scots, but it forged close links between the two countries, and perhaps its final manifestation, if not official, was the ineffectual French support for Bonnie Prince Charlie.

The most significant of David's successors was Alexander III, a strong King, married to a daughter of Henry III of England. In his reign, the Norwegians conceded control of the Western Islands, and the boundaries were established of a Scotland much as it is today. Traditionally, this was a golden age of peace and prosperity, a great time for the building of churches and castles, with an expansion of agriculture and trade. But the story of Alexander III has an unhappy ending. During the last ten years of his life, he lost his wife and all his children. He married again, hoping to produce an heir and to secure the succession. Late one night, riding home to his young wife, he fell from his horse in the darkness and was killed. His life was ended at the age of only forty-five, and since his widow failed to produce a child, his only heir was his little three year old granddaughter, Margaret of Norway. The "Maid of Norway" set sail for her Scottish possessions, but the poor child, one of the long series of royal minors who were pawns in the game of Scottish political history, died when she reached Orkney.

Her death caused a crisis between two powerful rival Anglo-Norman claimants, Robert Bruce the elder, and John Balliol, both descended from David I. Invited to help arbitrate between them, his appetite whetted by the conquest of Wales, the mighty warrior King Edward I of England was only too eager to intervene. Presided over by Edward, a specially appointed court chose John Balliol, the founder of the Oxford College, who was enthroned in 1292. Two years later, Edward peremptorily asserted his overlordship by demanding military service from the Scots. Balliol finally refused, but his decision was opposed by the Bruce family, who had large possessions over the Border. In 1295, reaffirming the French Alliance, Balliol invaded England, but two days later, Edward's large army of seasoned warriors marched across into Scotland. Many of the Scottish Barons, especially those with lands in England, were ready to pay homage. When Balliol learned that Robert Bruce and his son were among them, he confiscated their properties and gave them to his brother-in-law, John Comyn, Lord of Badenoch, known as the "Red Comyn."

In 1296, with terrible slaughter and brutality, Edward I took Berwick, defeated the Scots at Dunbar, and for several months laid waste Lowland Scotland. Among his booty was the famous Stone of Destiny, which found a new home in Westminster Abbey.

Resistance to the English was led by the heroic outlaw William Wallace, whose great victory was at Stirling Bridge in 1297. But the next year, Edward returned to Scotland with a punishing army of some 90,000 men, and Wallace was routed at Falkirk. He eluded capture until 1305, when he was tried, found guilty of treason and rebellion, and died by the recently devised refinement of hanging, drawing, and quartering.

At this stage, the Bruce family re-entered the story. This time with the grandson of the original claimant, Robert Bruce, Earl of Carrick. In 1299, Bruce had been appointed one of the Guardians of his country, another of them being the Red Comyn, who now considered himself the heir to the throne. Not surprisingly, there were hard feelings and friction, and during a violent quarrel at a conference in 1306, in an uncontrollable fit of anger, in front of the High Altar in the Greyfriars church at Dumfries, Bruce stabbed his rival to death. Seizing his moment, he went on to take the Castle, and to be solemnly enthroned as King of Scotland at Scone. From then onwards, he was dedicated to freeing his country from the English.

Whether or not the famous story of his gaining fresh courage from watching the persistence of a spider building her web is true, certainly he had great need of this quality in the next few years of disappointment and defeat. Always he fought back, and by 1313, he was acknowledged King by a great part of Scotland. By this time, he was no longer opposed by one of England's most ruthless and successful soldier kings, but by his effeminate and vacillating son, Edward II. As late as 1314, the English were still beseiged in Stirling Castle, and the army twenty thousand strong under the King, which had come to relieve the garrison, met Bruce and his five thousand Scots on the boggy field of Bannockburn.

Bruce had outmanoeuvred the English before the battle started, by choosing the high, dry ground, while the English cavalry floundered in the mud, falling into the turf-disguised pits which had been prepared for them; and by making sure that there was no space for the dreaded English archers to make the best use of their deadly weapons. The fighting raged fiercely all day, but by nightfall, the Scots had won a brilliant and decisive victory, and the English army had fled. After Bannockburn, there could no longer be any doubt about Scottish independence.

Robert Bruce was married twice. By his first wife, who was killed soon after he seized the throne, he had a daughter, Marjorie, who married Walter, High Steward of Scotland, and when he died of leprosy in 1329, by his second young wife, Elizabeth de Burgh, he left a little five year old son, David II. Bruce's last request was that his heart should be taken to the Holy Land on the Crusade he never had time to make, and hurled among the Saracens. But Sir James Douglas, to whom he entrusted this macabre mission, died on the journey, and the great patriot's heart was brought back and fittingly buried at Melrose Abbey. His body had already been interred at Dunfermline.

Not surprisingly, troubles broke out immediately on David II's accession, both with England and the Balliol family. The boy was brought up in France, and soon after his return to Scotland, was captured by the English at the Battle of Neville's Cross, and kept in captivity for eleven years. It was during this period that some of the Clans, in particular the house of Douglas, began building their power.

In 1357, David was ransomed and returned to his country for the remaining fourteen

years of his reign. He had no children, and his death ushered in the long dominion of the Stewarts.

The first significant Stewart king was James I, who, as a boy of twelve en route for security in France, was kidnapped by the English and kept a well-treated and privileged captive at the court of Henry IV. He went campaigning in France with Henry V and only after eighteen years of exile was allowed to return to his Kingdom. Understandably, he took a quick revenge on the Regent, the Duke of Albany, whom he blamed for failing to press for his release, and he and several members of his family were executed. James I was a poet, and he was a romantic who married Lady Joan Beaufort for love—"my heart became her thrall, for ever of free will." But he was also a strong king, a hard working executive with an eye for detail, who aimed at improving the royal revenues and curbing the power of the nobility.

He ruled successfully for thirteen years, but made many enemies. One night in 1437, as he was spending a quiet evening playing chess with his wife at Blackfriars House in Perth, a party of Atholl Stewarts and Grahams burst into the peaceful house. Unarmed and getting ready for bed, James tried to escape through the privy, but the exit was blocked. He defended himself bravely, but was soon overwhelmed and killed.

Another little boy came to the throne, his son James II, aged only seven. Like his father, he became the enemy of the barons who had manipulated his minority, in particular the leaders of Clan Douglas, who represented the most dangerous threat to his crown. But in 1452, at an angry meeting in Stirling, James took the law into his own hands and stabbed the Earl of Douglas to death. He himself was to die violently because of his passion for artillery, a memorial to which can still be seen at Edinburgh Castle—the great 15th century cannon *Mons Meg*. At the siege of Roxburgh, where he was attempting to drive the remnants of the English out of Scotland, he was killed by an explosion from a new type of cannon he was inspecting at the time.

James III came to the throne at the age of nine, and grew into a man born out of his time, a poor horseman, more interested in the arts than in warfare. Through his marriage to Margaret of Denmark and Norway, Scotland at last secured posession of the islands of Orkney and Shetland. He too failed to control his nobles and was killed in battle at Sauchieburn near Stirling, but luckily, by this time his son was almost of age.

James IV was handsome, strong, scholarly and musical, with a gift for languages. Much of his reign was spent in a finally unsuccessful attempt to bring the Highlands under peaceful royal control, but the clan system was too powerful for him. An extravagant enthusiast, he built palaces, of which Falkland and Linlithgow remain, and a white elephant of a battleship called *The Great Michael.* By marrying the daughter of the Tudor King Henry VII, he established the Stewart claim to the English throne, but when Henry VIII succeeded, relations between the two countries were strained. Henry was involved in a war with France, and the French claimed Scottish support for the Auld Alliance. The result was the most crushing and terrible defeat that Scotland was ever to know, on the tragic field of Flodden.

James IV died in the battle, leaving a baby son of only eighteen months to all the usual problems inherent in a long and disputed Regency. When he began to rule, James V showed some of the qualities of Henry VII, his Welsh grandfather, notably a proper appreciation of the power of money. By making two French marriages, he continued to antagonise his powerful uncle in England, and died shortly after his defeat at Solway Moss, seven days after the birth of his only surviving legitimate child, the girl who became the ill-fated Mary Queen of Scots.

"It cam wi' a lass and it'll gang wi' a lass," he is reputed to have said. Mary appears to have done her best to make her father's prediction come true, but in fact the lass the Stewart ruling line finally passed with was Queen Anne in 1714, and in 1603, Mary's son James VI became James I of England. After so many years of enmity and border quarrels, three countries were at last united under one crown, although for another century Scotland retained a separate Parliament until the violently opposed Act of Union was passed which resulted in Scottish Members sitting at Westminster instead of Edinburgh, and the end of an independent Scottish Parliament legislating for the benefit of the people of Scotland.

But already grave disturbances were brewing. For many ordinary people in Scotland the late sixteenth and the seventeenth centuries were lean and harsh times, even of famine, and there was much emigration to Ireland.

The enormous influence of John Knox, the fiery Calvinist preacher of St Giles, had prepared the ground for radical reforms in Scottish religious life that were to lead the country into extremes of Puritanism, and to the long struggle between the Presbyterian and the established Episcopal church. Knox was a virulent idealist, but no one would now doubt that he was right to believe that much of the wealth of the rich Catholic church might be put to better use in helping the poor and promoting education.

The small signs of unrest visible throughout the reign of the relatively easy-going James soon grew to alarming proportions under his obstinate son, Charles I. The Scottish National Covenant (those who signed it became known as the Covenanters), which as well as an expression of religious principles was a clarion call to rebellion against English interference in the Scottish church, and even aimed at establishing the Presbyterian church in England, was one of the events in the chain that led to Charles's overthrow and execution, and the period of Oliver Cromwell's Commonwealth or dictatorship, enforced in Sotland by General Monk.

But when it came to open opposition to a Scottish king, many found their loyalties divided, including that attractive character and brilliant soldier, John Graham, Marquess of Montrose. Although he was a Covenanter, he could not take up arms against his king, and he became commander of the Royalist forces in Scotland, leading a gallant army of mainly Highland and Irish Macdonalds against the forces led by Archibald Campbell, Earl of Argyll. Ill-equipped and outnumbered, under Montrose's outstanding leadership, his little army moved about the difficult country with unexpected speed, making inspired surprise attacks, and winning a series of brilliant victories. But eventually Montrose was defeated by the tendency of his troops to disappear on private looting expeditions, and betrayed by the terms under which the monarch he had fought for so bravely surrendered. After Charles's execution, Montrose's final battle at Carbisdale in support of the King's son ended in defeat, trial, and his own execution, and Charles II had to wait another ten years for his restoration.

When it came, the Restoration proved an unhappy period for the Covenanters who saw all they had gained slipping away and bitterly resisted attempts to reestablish the Episcopal church. When Archbishop Sharp was murdered, such terrible reprisals were taken by the government that the 1680s were known as "the killing time."

History almost seems to repeat itself in the career of Montrose's kinsman, John Graham of Claverhouse, Earl of Dundee, who was born in the year of Montrose's death and killed at about the same age, in his late thirties.

By this time, Charles II was dead and his Catholic brother James II and VII had failed

to maintain his royal authority. In his place, his nephew and daughter, William of
Orange and Mary had accepted the throne. The Scottish Parliament agreed to their
succession, but many remained loyal to James and his little son, afterwards the gloomy
Old Pretender. Among them was John Graham, of Claverhouse, first Viscount Dundee,
a ruthless professional soldier, who had fought in France and Holland, as well as against
the Covenanters in the cause of the Stewarts.

On William's accession, Dundee set off for the Highlands and called together the loyal
clans. General Mackay was sent to oppose him, and in Atholl just beyond the narrow
pass of Killiekrankie, the kilted, barefooted Highlanders swept silently down the hillside
and overwhelmed the government forces. But the victory which might have been a
beginning proved an end, for Dundee was killed in the battle, there was no one ready to

take his place, and the Highland forces melted away. General Mackay went on to build Fort William at Inverlochy, named in honour of the supplanting King, which, because it could be supplied from the sea, was a strategic point for holding the Highlands.

A pardon was offered to the chiefs who had fought against the government, provided they swore an oath of allegiance before 1st January 1692. MacIan Macdonald of Glencoe, dilatory in the first place, held up by a snowstorm, and delayed by the absence of the Sheriff, was a few days late. His supposed omission was reported, and William III was persuaded to sign a document authorising the annihilation of the Glencoe Macdonalds. Some apologists claim he never read it, but that at best is a poor excuse.

Only too ready to take the offensive against their hereditary enemies, the Campbells were appointed to the dreadful task. With their well known record of changing sides for their own benefit, the Campbells were unpopular with most of the other Highland Clans. But the Macdonalds welcomed them in friendship, and for nearly two weeks they enjoyed their hospitality in that remote mountain glen. One morning in the early hours, they rose to massacre their hosts. Thirty-eight were murdered, and of those that escaped many starved and perished in the winter snows. It was a tale of treachery and horror which illustrates all the worst aspects of Clan life—violence, feuding, and revenge. At the same time, the positive virtues of the old Clansmen must also be remembered, of loyalty, courage, unique tradition and culture.

The long saga of the Highland clans was soon to come to an end with the defeat of the Young Pretender, Bonnie Prince Charlie, at Culloden in 1746. With the last of the Stewarts departed the old life of the Highlands, under the vindictive and brutal reprisals carried out by the aptly nicknamed "Butcher" Cumberland, the brother of George II, the second of the new line of Hanoverian kings who had succeeded Queen Anne.

Every attempt was made to break up the old loyalties and associations; the bearing of arms and the wearing of Highland dress were forbidden, and many were exiled from their homes. When these harsh restrictions were withdrawn in 1782, a revival began of the more peaceful clan traditions which continues today. An important step was taken to preserve and inject new life into Gaelic culture as recently as 1972 by the inauguration of the International Clan Gathering and Ceilidh (a cheerful gathering for singing and story telling).

In 1822, plump and wearing discreet flesh coloured pantaloons under his kilt, George IV paid a state visit to Scotland—the first reigning monarch to visit his northern kingdom since Charles II. This visit, when Highland chiefs were asked to attend the court in their tartans, together with the publication of the work known as the Vestiarium Scoticum by the two Sobieski Stuart brothers, who without the slightest foundation claimed to be grandchildren of Bonnie Prince Charlie, triggered off an explosion in the production of tartans. Undoubtedly the handwoven cloth, and the simpler and more sombrely coloured patterns associated with districts and clans, had existed for centuries—long before the first recorded mention in 1538 of the purchase of three ells of "Helande Tertane" for some trews for James V. But with the growth of the textile industry and the introduction of brighter dyes in the 19th century, more complicated patterns were designed, until the tartans achieved the enormous variety maintained and sold throughout the world today.

Economically and culturally Scotland made great progress in the 18th and 19th centuries: in the movement towards religious toleration; the establishment of law; the growth of the educational system, and the greater achievements of the universities, particularly in medicine; in literature, art, and science; in better methods of banking; in civil engineering; in the improvement of agriculture, fisheries, and industry—textiles, iron and coal; and although Scotland no longer had its own parliament, there was much vigorous political activity. In the late 19th century Keir Hardy founded the Independent Labour Party, and between 1894 and 1931, Scotland provided the United Kingdom with six prime ministers—Lord Rosebery, Balfour, Campbell Bannerman, Asquith, Bonar Law, and Ramsay Macdonald.

Unfortunately, the standard of living of the workers did not improve correspondingly during this period, and there were grave problems in housing, sanitation, nutrition, and general health. The rising population of the Highlands caused economically sound, but bitterly unpopular, movements to clear unproductive areas for large scale sheep farms.

Naturally people resented being dispossessed, sometimes it seemed only in order that gentlemen might come to Scotland to shoot deer, and the economics of rents and profits were so unfair that many tenants who wished only to stay on the land they loved were forced to leave to survive. There was much emigration to the big cities, principally Glasgow, and to countries further afield like America and Australia.

Until the 1914-18 war, the greatest single contribution towards Scotland's prosperity had been made by shipbuilding. But the world-wide depression which followed hit this industry particularly hard, and there was widespread unemployment and suffering which was not substantially alleviated until the need for rearmament for the second World War.

Since World War II, although the population has remained static because of emigration—the response to the call of a new country has always been a Scottish characteristic and the Scots made a tremendous contribution to the establishment of the British Empire—the pattern has begun to change. Industry has diversified, living standards have risen, attention is being paid to the development of the Highlands, after two hundred and seventy years of political union, people are actively pressing for political independence, and there is the new economic potential of the North Sea oil . . .

Scotland, a beautiful country with a fascinating past, faces a challenging and exciting future.

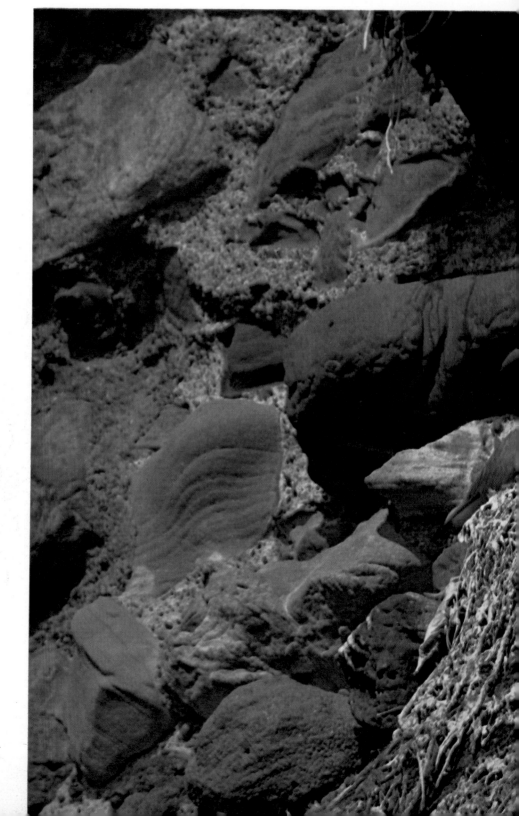

The Birds of Scotland/David Fisher

No national boundary in the world can ever hope to exclude birds from entering a country, or to restrain them from leaving it, when the fancy takes them. As free citizens of the freest kingdom on earth they traverse seas and continents at will, presenting no passports, requesting no permission to land.

In what sense, then, can any bird be called a 'bird of Scotland'? None is showing the slightest sign of developing tartan plumage, of course, but for all that, Scotland can lay stronger claim than most other countries to being the unique habitat of more than one species. Amongst others, the golden eagle, greenshank, dotterell and the St Kilda wren scarcely need to apply for naturalisation papers.

Reasons for Scotland's popularity both as visiting-ground and breeding-place with the birds are not far to seek. Human habitations are mostly concentrated in relatively small, well-defined areas, leaving broad tracts of sparsely populated country available to wild creatures. An immense variety of habitat exists within Scotland's borders: cliffs and the sea, river and mountain, fresh-water and sea lochs, sandy shores and mud flats, forest-clad hills and wooded glens; and all around, a multitude of islands. Considering the sheer range of species that the wealth of terrain is able to support and to shelter, you would be unlucky to pass through the Scottish countryside and not see at least one bird unfamiliar to you, even if you never left the road.

What can you expect to see, though, when you do leave the beaten track, and is the show worth the effort you make to watch it? Perhaps you really need a great deal of knowledge about birds, or an expert guide or expensive fieldglasses in order to get the genuine, ornithological kick out of bird-watching? Of course all these things help you to enjoy the pursuit, but none of them can make up in the slightest degree for a keen, natural interest; for that divine gift of curiosity. Everywhere in the nature reserves you will meet men and women whose heads are stuffed with enough bird-lore to fill an encyclopedia apiece, but they are not to be found locked away in libraries, writing down all that they know. Far from it. Most of the time you will find them out in the open, on the lookout for something they have not seen before. Enhanced though it may be by their learning and experience, the pleasure they seek is identical to that the most amateur observer can find: the feeling of Look! What's that bird? What's it doing? Why? "The creature hath a purpose, and his eyes are bright with it." That brief borrowing from Keats epitomises the fascination of observing wild life: the level of observation is unimportant.

A totally reasonable answer to the question: where can you see birds in Scotland? would be 'Everywhere', but the country abounds in places where the opportunities to see particular species are especially good, either because of a natural concentration or by reason of the protection offered by a nature reserve. In the Western Lowlands, there are the Threave Wildfowl Refuge (Kirkcudbright), the cormorants on Castle Loch (Wigtown), Ailsa Craig off the coast of Ayr and the Solway Firth. The Eastern Lowlands and the Borders offer St Abb's Head, Dunstanburgh and the islands of the Firth of Forth, for seabirds in general, Lamb for cormorants and Eyebroughy for eiders, which go there in the moulting season (the tail-end of the summer). Eiders also frequent Bass Rock, which is a favourite breeding-ground of several thousand gannets into the bargain. The Orkneys and the Hebrides in the North West afford the inaccessibility that attracts the rarer species, though the neighbouring North West Highlands of the mainland are similarly favoured in that respect. Some birds that shun all other parts of Britain as breeding places make their homes regularly in the North-East Highlands. This region boasts the osprey eyrie at Loch Garten, for example. More gregarious species are to be seen at such sites as the Hatton Castle Rookery in Aberdeenshire, reputed to have over 9,000 nests. In the Ythan Valley estuary there usually lives a colony of eider ducks, whilst at Aviemore in the Spey valley there is perhaps the largest bird-watching centre in all Scotland.

Remarkable though the greater collections of bird life may be, and however natural to the regions where they occur, they each require a fairly generous allocation of time to allow the visitor to do true justice to their wealth of interest. Civic or tourist information centres can always tell you which of them are accessible from wherever you happen to be. Even if you are only passing through the countryside, or doing a little fishing or taking a holiday on a farm, there are still countless birds to be seen. What kinds to keep an eye open for depends on the type of terrain you are in. A good deal of overlapping is bound to exist, of course, by reason of the supreme adaptability of many species, but broadly the picture is as follows.

SEASHORE BIRDS

Perhaps better known for its down than for its appearance, the eider is a not uncommon sight along flat shores, which provide it with the ever-open whelk-stall it needs to give it its diet: exclusively shellfish. The eider is a large bird (some two feet from bill to tail), or rather two birds, drake and duck having strikingly different plumages. He is white on top and black beneath, she a well-camouflaged brown for protection on her nest, which is always on the ground very near the level of high tide. Outside the breeding season, you are more likely to see eiders riding the seas like corks, totally fearless of the roughest water. By contrast, the smaller scoters hate choppy sea, preferring to dive for their food in the calmer stretches well inshore. Look out for a coal-black drake and a dark-brown duck. She has lighter cheek-patches, and both have rather pointed bills.

If you are very lucky, you may spot a great northern diver, a very large bird with black head and neck and gull-like bill. Half again as big as the eider, this diver (as its name suggests) virtually lives in the sea, where its underwater swimming capability enables it to catch absolutely any creature not too big to be swallowed at a gulp. It is rare for the diver to breed in Scotland, but from October to May there is a sporting chance of sighting one inland, seeking shelter from a gale or a storm.

A walk in any grassy or soft, bare ground near to water, be it sea, loch or river, may well bring you to within a short distance of a ringed plover's nest, at any time from May to July. Not that you are likely to find it, but if you notice a little bird something under blackbird-size, with a black-and-white collar band, dragging a 'broken' white-barred wing along the ground, you can be sure that it is trying to distract your attention from its brood in the turf nearby. On an unfrequented beach, ringed plovers are often seen in considerable flocks, scampering madly about on their bright yellow legs, stopping every now and then to pick titbits from the sand.

Gulls in great variety you will find in most parts of Britain, but you are not likely to find an arctic tern outside Scotland. Distinguished by its red bill and black cap, and by its forked tail, this graceful, grey-and-white fisherman is noted for ferocity in defending the nest, which is a makeshift hollow in open ground. Amongst Scotland's most appreciative tourists, the Arctic tern is oddly named, for it spends its winters fishing the Antarctic seas.

Should there be oystercatchers about, you will be left in little doubt about their presence, since they invariably advertise it energetically. On the seashore, these large and handsome black-and-white waders use their workmanlike, long, orange, crowbar bills to prise open the shellfish that form their staple diet, though, like the gulls, they are perfectly well able to make a good living inland, subsisting on insects and worms. Nesting time is early in the year (April/May), and brings into prominence the oystercatchers' social co-operation system. Any attack on any of their nests results in a concerted sortie by all the other oystercatchers in the neighbourhood. Not surprisingly, fledgling losses are few, and the species thrives.

SEABIRDS OF CLIFF AND ROCK

So many of Scotland's mainland and island coasts feature cliffs remote from human habitations, that its seabirds and other coastal cliff-dwelling species are almost spoilt for choice as to places where they can live unfettered lives. Some there are that literally live over the open sea, visiting the land but briefly to rear their young. These are the Manx shearwaters (that can find their way back to a cliff-top nest hole after flights of several thousand miles, usually landing in pitch darkness), the magnificent gannets (with their six-foot wing span), the fulmars (masters of the art of gliding) and the two species of petrel. Both the storm petrel and Leach's petrel nest like the shearwaters in disused burrows, mainly on the more isolated islands off Scotland's North and West coasts. Leach's petrel lives by fishing the open sea, but the storm petrel has earned itself the nickname of 'Mother Cary's chicken' by its habit of following boats.

Remote cliff areas, where they can live relatively unmolested lives, are giving threatened species like the puffin a sporting chance of survival. This picturesque little auk is fascinating to watch in the spring and the summer when it comes inshore to breed: whether bobbing about in the water, diving for fish or speeding arrow-like for home, its chunky red wedge of a bill gripping a writhing catch, wings beating so rapidly as to be almost invisible. Puffins winter at sea, but even there they are largely at the mercy of gulls and of other professional muggers like the skuas, so it is to be hoped that man never encroaches on their Scottish habitats as he has on their English ones.

Quite a few species like to live near the sea and to take food from it, even though they may never enter the water to fish. One such bird is the rock dove, original ancestor of pigeons tame and town. Easily identified by a green and purple 'bib', white rump and black bars on its wings, this wild member of the tamest family of birds now lives quietly in isolated colonies around the west and north coasts of Scotland. Unlike most other species, it becomes more difficult to watch them in the breeding season than in the open, since they nest in hidden caves and fissures in the rock. A more extrovert seaside denizen is the rock-pipit. Despite his grey-brown drabness and sparrowlike stature, the male rock-pipit has a delightful habit that makes him entertaining to observe. It can make a welcome change from listening to the screeches of the sea-going fraternity to come on this little songster of the shore. He takes off almost vetically, giving a fair imitation of a skylark, his song quickening in tempo up to the climax of his ascent, turning into a tuneful, gentle warble as he planes smoothly downward.

Sea cliffs, especially those bordering islands, form natural sanctuaries for that greatly depleted race of predators, the peregrines. They owe their reduction in numbers entirely to the activities of mankind: shot in earlier years for killing domestic fowl, victims today of poisonous pesticides. Certainly their decline cannot be attributed to any lack of survival technique on their part. Both male (tiercel) and female (falcon) are deadly killers, catching birds in the air and small animals on the ground with equal ease. Like miniature eagles, they cruise high to scan the world below for victims, on sighting which they 'stoop' for the kill in spectacular, swallow-speed dives. You are more likely to see the birds in silhouette against the sky than nearby, but if you do get a close look, you will be able to tell tiercel from falcon, as she is much bigger. Both have the typical hawk's head, long tapering wings and long tail, and a flecked and barred underside, but he has a slate-blue back whereas hers is brown. An odd couple, but they must get along well together, for they mate for life.

BIRDS OF THE INLAND REGIONS
Woodland birds form a striking contrast to those which have chosen to live in the unobstructed air over the sea. In the constricted spaces and filtered light among the trees, there have evolved short wings, eyes placed to give good rearward vision, delicate claws and abbreviated tails. Strangely enough, the woodcock, which embodies most of these developments, was originally a wading bird. Often hunted for the table, the woodcock has become a wary fugitive from human kind, so you are most likely to catch a glimpse of one surprised from its hiding place: a red-brown flash dodging swiftly between branches back into cover.

Deciduous woods are the woodcock's domain, but the more truly Scottish residents are to be found in the pinewoods, where the black grouse and the capercaillie live. Think of them as wild chickens and wild turkeys, respectively, and you will easily recognise at least the males of the two species if you see them. In the spring, male capercaillies indulge in enthusiastic sparring matches with other cocks. Both involve much displaying of tail feathers and spectacular leaps in the air, and the fights take place on an organised, communal basis. Probably they are ritual elimination contests, designed to keep the males appropriately aggressive. If so, the idea has worked well in the capercaillie's case: cocks of that species show no fear of man or beast when guarding their territory.

Generous expanses of mountain and moorland make Scotland a sanctuary for many birds which, if not all rarities, have become somewhat rarer outside Scotland than in it. Hooded crows ('Hoodies') fall into this category, but like golden plovers and ravens they are still relatively numerous. Britain's shrinking species which find Scotland a major stronghold against extinction are the little brown dotterel (now confined to the Cairngorms); that dainty wader, the greenshank (Highlands, Skye and outer Hebrides); the mountain-dwelling ptarmigan; hen harriers and golden eagles. Doubtless there are still pockets of some of these breeding outside the British Isles, but it would be a sad day for Britain when the last wild bird was driven to extinction. May Scotland's shining example in the preservation of free country in which they may live and breed inspire emulation outside its borders, so that the sun need never rise to an empty sky.

Scotland is rich in royal associations, and it would be difficult to imagine a more romantic and dramatic capital than Edinburgh.

The rock from which Edinburgh Castle dominates the city is volcanic in origin, like its neighbour, Arthur's seat. Rising suddenly above the surrounding land, from time immemorial it must have been used as a place of refuge and shelter. It is recorded that in the 7th century, Edwin of Northumbria was rebuilding the castle there, and certainly King Malcolm III and his saintly wife Margaret made it their home. In their reign was begun the building of St Margaret's Chapel, one of the few examples of Norman architecture in Scotland, and the oldest building still in use in Edinburgh.

It was Margaret's youngest son, King David I, who founded the Abbey of Holyrood, as legend has it, because of a hunting accident when, grasping for the antlers of a fierce stag which was attacking him, he found in his hands instead a cross that put the animal to flight. All that remains now of the Abbey, where most of the marriages of the Stewart kings took place, is the ruined nave.

When James IV made Edinburgh his capital, he converted the guest house of the

Abbey into his Palace of Holyroodhouse, although it was not completed until many years later in the reign of Charles II. It is still used for State occasions when the Queen is in residence.

Edinburgh Castle and Holyroodhouse are linked by the great thoroughfare known as the Royal Mile, which includes the Esplanade, Castle Hill, Lawnmarket, Parliament Square, High Street and Canongate. Princes Street, on the other side of the Castle, was part of the elegant and classically designed New Town, and not completed until 1805. As we know it today, Edinburgh is a beautiful, sophisticated city. But it must have been a very different place when the widowed Mary Queen of Scots returned there in August 1561 from all the luxury and grandeur she had enjoyed as Queen of France. She was only eighteen at that time, tall, accomplished, gay, and radiantly attractive. Mary was a Catholic, and the reformer John Knox was thundering his warnings of doom from the church of St Giles. She was never quite sure whom she could trust. Wealthy France was enjoying the music and poetry of the Renaissance, while poor Scotland was still existing in the harsh world of the middle ages. Her new Kingdom must have seemed a bleak,

bewildering place. Even forty years later, her son James was astonished at the comfortable and gracious way of life he found in England on his accession, compared to the Spartan regime he had endured as King of Scotland.

Both Edinburgh Castle and Holyroodhouse are full of memories of the courageous young Queen who failed to keep her crown, but whose son was destined to reign over the three countries of the United Kingdom. She fell in love and was married to her cousin Lord Darnley in the Chapel Royal at Holyrood. Soon she became pregnant, but her love did not long survive her marriage. Darnley, an ambitious, degenerate youth, who wanted to rule like a King, became obsessively jealous of Mary's preference for the company of her artistic Italian secretary, David Rizzio. One evening, as she was enjoying a quiet intimate supper with Rizzio and a few friends, her husband and a party of conspirators violently entered the little crimson and green room and with many brutal strokes stabbed the Italian to death. The room, and the spot where his murdered body lay, can still be seen.

Miraculously, Mary did not lose her baby, and James was born in a small, dark room in Edinburgh Castle. He had the lucky caul over his head, and was a fine and healthy child.

A few months later, his father was dead, blown out of the house he was occupying at the Kirk o'Field by a large explosion of gunpowder. Later, on a famous November 5th, James himself was to be more fortunate. Darnley's death has always been and must remain a mystery. The scene of the crime is somewhere near the Old Buildings of the university, on the corner of College and Nicholas Streets.

Few Scots regretted Darnley, but when Mary agreed to marry that tough adventurer with an eye to the main chance, James Hepburn, Earl of Bothwell, then understandably they rejected her. The twice widowed Queen may have thought she had found a strong protector, but Bothwell proved an even more disastrous choice than Darnley. They parted forever after only three months; knowing he dared not remain in Scotland, Bothwell fled to Denmark and for the rest of his life remained in prison, eventually dying insane. For all the history and romance that has been written about them, no-one can ever be sure whether their marriage sprang from a brief but irresistible passion, or merely ambition on his side, and on hers desperation and expediency.

Mary was imprisoned on the island castle of Loch Leven and forced to abdicate in favour of her baby son. While she was there, she miscarried of the twins fathered by Bothwell and was extremely ill. But ten months later, her charm enabled her to make a successful escape. On her way to Dumbarton Castle, still held by her supporters, at Langside near Glasgow, she made a last forlorn and gallant attempt to fight for her throne. When she saw that all was lost, taking the most critical of her many wrong decisions, she fled to imprisonment and eventual execution in Elizabeth's England.

Other places especially associated with Mary are: the Palace of Linlithgow, where she was born; Falkland, the fine palace completed by her father, which became a favourite royal retreat where Mary, who was a brilliant horsewoman, particularly enjoyed the sports of hunting and hawking; Traquair House, where she stayed with Darnley, and some of her letters, her rosary, her crucifix, and her little son's cradle may still be seen; Dunbar, where she escaped with the wretched and unstable Darnley after Rizzio's murder, riding at night a distance of twenty-five miles when she was six months pregnant and was the castle to which Bothwell forcibly abducted her; the grim fortress of Hermitage Castle where she once visited Bothwell, who had been seriously wounded in a

Border foray, making another marathon ride of fifty miles from Jedburgh and back in a day; and Stirling Castle, where as a baby of nine months she had been crowned, and where twenty-five years later she spent a happy day with her ten-months-old son, little thinking it was the last time she would ever see him.

Undoubtedly the most glamorous and best known of all the Royal Scots, Mary has captivated hosts of admirers through the centuries and inspired many writers.

Second only to hers is the appeal of the Stewart who never reigned, Bonnie Prince Charlie. In his brief campaign to win back the throne for his father, which started successfully and ended at Culloden in utter disaster, the tall, fair, handsome young man impressed himself forever on the Scottish romantic imagination.

Perhaps the most exciting moment was at the very beginning, when he waited uneasily with only two companies of MacDonalds at the rallying point in the rugged valley of Glenfinnan. He had almost begun to despair when he heard in the distance the sound of men marching. First came Lochiel with eight hundred Camerons, and soon many other chiefs with their loyal clansmen. The Stewart royal standard was held aloft by the Marquis of Tullibardine, cheers resounded, and the adventure had begun which was to lead them to Edinburgh, a great victory at Prestonpans, and as far south as Derby, before the turn of the tide and the final defeat. Charles never entered Edinburgh Castle, but he did hold court at Holyroodhouse. He even gave a ball, and (a striking figure in his tartan coat and scarlet breeches) caused many a flutter in the hearts of the Lowland ladies.

Although he had a Scottish mistress, Clementina Walkinshaw, by whom he had his only well authenticated child, Charlotte (whom he later created Duchess of Albany), the lady whose name is forever linked with his is Flora MacDonald. The brave lass who dressed him as her maid and with £30,000 on his head, an enormous sum in those days, helped him to escape from the Isle of South Uist to Skye, from whence he was eventually able to make his final flight to France.

"Will ye no come back again?" the song beseeches. But the bitterly disappointed Prince took to the bottle, and it was just as well he didn't return. Paradoxically enough, Flora and her husband, who spent many years in America, fought hard for the Hanoverian George III in the War of Independence.

An earlier Stewart, Charles II, the Merry Monarch, during his battles with Cromwell shortly after his father's execution, spent some dismal months in Scotland in the uncongenial and self-righteous company of the Covenanters. He put a good face on it, and it is said once managed to sit through six consecutive sermons. His reward was a splendid coronation at Scone, but he was always to look back on his sojourn in Scotland with horror. Perhaps he was not the only one to resent the prevailing grimness and gloom, for when the news of his restoration reached Edinburgh, some 300 dozen glasses were broken at the Market Cross after drinking His Majesty's health.

Charles II was the last reigning king to visit Scotland until the State visit of George IV in 1822. The King who had waited so long to inherit, much better known as the Prince Regent, sailed up from Greenwich to the Firth of Forth. He stayed outside Edinburgh at Dalkeith Palace, but Holyroodhouse Palace was used for the splendid State occasions. The visit was brilliantly stage-managed by Sir Walter Scott and was a great success. At last a Hanoverian king had been accepted by the majority of his Scottish subjects.

But the monarch who carried on a life-long love affair with Scotland was Queen Victoria. She and her beloved Albert made the first of their many visits in 1842, when

Albert wrote approvingly, "The country is full of beauty of a severe and grand character perfect for sport and the air remarkably clear." They loved the Highlands so much that in 1848 they decided to make a permanent holiday home at Balmoral, beautifully situated on the river Dee with some 40,000 acres, mostly of deer forest. The original castle, first mentioned in 1484, was too small for the demands of the royal household, and Prince Albert, who had purchased the property, commissioned William Smith, an Aberdeen architect, to design the new turreted and buttressed castle of pale grey granite. When it was finished, with small regard for history, the old castle was pulled down. On their first visit, the Queen recorded, "The new house looks beautiful . . . An old shoe was thrown after us into the house, for good luck, when we entered the hall. The house is charming: the rooms delightful; the furniture, papers, everything perfection."

The Queen and her family all loved the countryside and the forthright manners of the Highland people. They wore tartan; they learned Scottish dancing; Albert even had a little shot at learning Gaelic; they walked, they went pony trekking, they salmon fished

and Albert shot stag; they enjoyed the traditional games and dancing at the Braemar Gathering; the Queen wrote her journal and sketched.

Not all the court was so enthusiastic, for Balmoral had its inconveniences; the family regime was strict and conventional; the house was considered chilly and draughty, not everyone liked the wallpapers as much as the Queen did, it seemed a long way from London, and quite often it rained.

It was at Balmoral that Queen Victoria found her faithful and indispensable John Brown who, after Albert's death, was promoted from one of the royal gillies to the Queen's personal servant. He looked after her horses, on the box of her carriage always accompanied her on her outings, and in his rough, blunt way made her feel cherished and protected. On her Highland picnics, the Queen always said no one ever made a cup of tea like Mr Brown, no doubt due to the fact that he treated his monarch on equal terms with himself, and added a good dram of whisky, And if he sometimes showed signs of having taken a little too much, in his case, the Queen was prepared to overlook it.

In 1868, the Queen published a little book, *Leaves from a Journal of our Life in the Highlands,* a simple record which illustrates the relief and happiness she found with her family in such beautiful surroundings, remote from the pressure and anxiety of her great office. Feelings that are surely shared by our own Queen and her family today.

Now, our Royal family is linked to Scotland not only by affection but by the ties of blood, for Elizabeth the Queen Mother is a Scot, the daughter of the Earl of Strathmore. Her ancestral home is the magnificent Castle of Glamis, twelve miles north of Dundee, which was rebuilt during the 17th century and with its round towers and turrets has the graceful and elegant air of a French château. The Queen Mother now has her own Scottish castle at Mey.

One of the most dramatically situated of all Scottish castles with royal associations is Dunnottar in Kincardineshire. Perched high above the sea in a seemingly impregnable position, it is now an imposing ruin. King Donald fought the Norse invaders from this stronghold in the ninth century, and Charles II chose it as a hiding place for the Royal Regalia of Scotland. When the Castle surrendered after an eight months siege, the Regalia had been smuggled out and buried under the altar of the parish church. These treasures, including the Crown of Scottish gold, remodelled by James V in 1540, studded with pearls, diamonds and other stones; the sceptre; and the sword of State, are now displayed at Edinburgh Castle in the Crown Room.

Edinburgh is one of the world's great capital cities, full of beauty, historic interest, and dramatic contrast. The Castle and Holyroodhouse Palace must always be principal attractions, but there is much more to impress and delight the tourist, both in the ancient huddle of the Old Town, and the classic elegance of the New.

The Old Town, like Topsy, just "growed", but when the city began to expand beyond its walls towards the end of the 18th century, the New Town was specially designed and planned by the young architect, James Craig.

In the heart of the Old Town is the church of St Giles, the High Kirk of Scotland, which has a long and violent history. The original 12th century church was largely destroyed by fire during the English invasion in 1385. Rebuilt during the 14th and 15th centuries, it has a fine "crown" steeple. Some less fortunate work was carried out during the early 19th century, when the only remainder of its ancient past, a richly carved Norman doorway, was demolished. The Chapel of the Most Ancient and Most Noble Order of the Thistle was designed by Sir Robert Lorimer early in the 20th century, and contains some fine carving.

John Knox became Minister of the Kirk in 1559, and during his ministry much of the beautiful interior and many treasures of the church vanished or were destroyed, including the most sacred relic, the armbone of St Giles, patron saint of the poor and crippled. In July 1637, the church was the scene of a rebellious uproar when the congregation violently disapproved of Archbishop Laud's new liturgy, which Charles I wanted to impose, and stools were hurled at poor Dean Hannay who was reading the service. Soon after this incident, the National Covenant was composed. The mutilated body of gallant Montrose lies at rest in St Giles, and there is a monument to Robert Louis Stevenson who died in Samoa, far from his native city.

In the High Street, not far from the great church he did so much to transform, is the picturesque house where John Knox is believed to have lived during the 1560s. Of particular interest in the Lawn Market are two 17th century buildings, Lady Stair's House, now a Museum, and Gladstone's Land, which has been finely restored and is now the property of the National Trust for Scotland, and the headquarters of the Saltire Society, which does so much to preserve the country's many valuable traditions.

What was once the seat of Scotland's Parliament now houses the law courts, and although the building dates from 1640 and has a fine hammerbeam roof, the exterior was altered, many would say spoiled, in 1829. It contains some interesting portraits, including some fine Raeburns. Earlier Parliaments were held in the Great Hall at the Castle.

Among other places of interest in the Old Town are Canongate Church and Tolbooth; the Grassmarket, the scene of many executions; Greyfriars Church, and the university.

In the different age and atmosphere of the New Town, most people make first for Princes Street, which gazes across the green gulf of the gardens to the heights of the Castle, and must be one of the most strikingly beautiful shopping centres in the world. Many of the spacious streets, squares, and terraces show the classical influence of Robert Adam, who designed Charlotte Square and the new university buildings. The Register House was also built from Adam's designs, and is the home of Scottish public records dating from the 13th century to the present day.

Conspicuously out of character with the prevailing Georgian restraint and style is the Victorian Gothic monument to Sir Walter Scott in East Princes Street Gardens, which includes statuettes of sixty-four of the best known characters from his novels and a seated figure of the author with his faithful deerhound, Maida, at his feet.

As well as a writer of genius and a fine human character, Scott was a great patriot, and we may be sure that nothing would have delighted him more than the creation of the Festival by which Edinburgh is known throughout the world today.

The Edinburgh International Festival of the Arts was inaugurated in 1947 in the bleak austere days after the war. It was an act of faith in the endurance of the human spirit in the face of violence and calamity. It made a brilliant and exciting beginning, and held ever since during the last two weeks of August and the first of September, has remained the most stimulating celebration of music, opera, and drama, both old and new.

Art has no frontiers, and the continuing numbers of overseas enthusiasts flying in from every direction each year constantly reaffirm that the Edinburgh Festival belongs to the world. Yet one of its most constantly popular and thrilling events is the Military Tattoo, which takes place on the romantic floodlit esplanade of the Castle, and is uniquely and movingly Scottish.

One glance at the map of the tortured coastline is enough to show how inseparable Scottish life must be from the sea. Everywhere deep tidal arms invade the land, fissured into the heart of moor and mountain like pulsating veins, so that few Scots can be born more than 40 miles from salt water. Only 25 miles separate the Firth of Forth from the Firth of Clyde and the only border not washed by the sea is the 60 miles shared with England. Add to this the country's 787 islands and the dependence of generations of Scots on their mastery of the sea becomes apparent.

Beating against gaunt, jagged cliffs, the highest in the British Isles, guarded by offlying stacks and skerries, and ensnared by treacherous tide rips like the notorious ones of the Pentland Firth and Corryvreckan, she has been a hard mistress, and the demands of the sea, as much as those of terrain, have moulded over the centuries the independent spirit and unique character of Scotland.

It was from the sea that the early invasions came. The Roman legions had come by land and largely failed, but in 563 AD St Columba landed from Ireland on the tiny island of Iona with an army of 12 monks and in the next 34 years conquered much of Scotland and Northern England with his message. While converting the various little kingdoms to Christianity, Columba was also instrumental in starting the process of unification which led to the emergence of modern Scotland.

Then, from the other direction and rather less peacefully, came the dragon-prowed longships of the Vikings. The 200 year saga of pillage and plunder which followed left large parts of Scotland subject to the Norwegian crown, a state of affairs which continued into the 15th century when Shetland and Orkney became firmly and finally Scots. Shetlanders still carry on the tradition of their sea raiding ancestors in the custom of Up-helli-Aa. Every January a torchlight procession hauls a model Viking ship through the streets of Lerwick to set it on fire amid general jollification and the singing of Norse songs handed down for a thousand years.

A later invasion, or at least an attempted one, has left another surviving legacy in Scottish waters. When the Spanish Armada was defeated in the English Channel in 1588 and scattered by storms, many of the ships which tried to escape northabout were wrecked on the Scottish coast. One, the *Florida,* or as some records say the *San Francisco,* limped to Tobermory on the Isle of Mull seeking food, water and repairs. There she blew up and sank, as a result it is said of some skulduggery on the part of the MacLeans, taking to the bottom the treasure chest of the Armada containing gold which more conservative writers value at £500,000.

Attempts to find the alleged Armada gold have been going on since 1640. One Duke of Argyll, whose family claim an hereditary right to the treasure, brought over a diving bell from Sweden but Charles the Second sent a man o'war to put a stop to operations. It didn't succeed, but neither did the Duke and hopeful seekers, spurred on even more now by modern aqua lung diving methods, have been searching the sea off Tobermory ever since.

Mention of Scotland and the sea for almost any sassenach is certain to evoke at least one response. If they know nothing else of Scotland beyond the kilt and the bagpipe they will know "Over The Sea to Skye", the haunting melody which tells the story of the Young Pretender, fleeing after his defeat at Culloden. The sea the song refers to is that stretch between the islands of Benbecula and Skye known as the Little Minch. In truth the 'bonny boat' would hardly have been able to 'speed like a bird on the wing' because the crew had a hard row in gales and squally weather, not daring to hoist sail

for fear of being spotted by Navy sloops which were in sight just to the North.

The drama of the '45 was in fact as much one of the sea as of the glens and heather. The six months following Culloden were one long relentless game of hide and seek among the rocks, lochs and swirling tides of the West Highland coast. Between one island and another and back again to some mainland hill fastness slipped the fugitive prince. Hot on his heels at every move came the Navy's sloops, *Baltimore, Terror, Greyhound* and *Furnace,* sixth raters sent because ships of the line, even frigates, could not handily negotiate these tortuous waters. At every township they landed boats seeking for news of the Pretender, flogging any suspected of succouring him. And dodging the sloops, four or five privateers, financed by the French government, equally intent on exploring every creek and islet, hoping to snatch the Prince and land him safely in Brittany before King George's ships caught up.

One day in May 1746 the *Baltimore* and *Terror* surprised two of the privateers, the latter both more powerful, in Loch nan Uamh which divides Arisaig from Moidart, where Charles Edward had landed with such brave hopes ten months before. There ensued a bloody if inconclusive battle, the sound of the six hour cannonade reverberating round the hills. It was thus at sea, rather than on Culloden Moor, that the last shots of the Rising, and of all Stuart aspirations, were ultimately fired.

On board one of these Navy sloops hunting the Pretender was a tall, good looking midshipman on his first voyage, 15 year old Adam Duncan, son of the Provost of Dundee. In maturity he stood 6ft 4ins with a build and strength proportionate, an amiable, devastatingly handsome giant whom the women of Chatham ran to their windows to see pass by.

As Admiral Duncan, the hero of Camperdown, he gave Britain one of the great victories of the French Revolutionary Wars and gave historians two favourite legends. The first concerns the occasion when the fleet with which he was blockading the Dutch off the Texel was reduced to two ships because the other eleven, embroiled in the Mutiny of the Nore, had refused to sail. With Scots cunning he hid his weakness by signalling to an imaginary fleet, which the enemy assumed to be lying just below the horizon. The second story arose when even this two ship blockade was threatened by disaffection aboard the 50 gun *Adamant.* Having himself rowed over from his flagship *Venerable,* Admiral Duncan addressed the men and asked if any disputed his authority. When one militant shouted "I do" Duncan lunged forward, plucked him from the crowd and with one hand held him suspended over the ship's side, asking if "anyone now dares deprive me of my command?" It was the end of the mutiny in that ship.

Duncan was one of the many Scottish officers who made their contribution to British maritime power in the 18th and 19th centuries. For them the sea was the road to adventure, glory and possibly a fortune in prize money. For hundreds of thousands of fellow Scots in the same period it was a road of misery and despair. These were the pitiful emigrants, driven from their homelands by the great Highland clearances, dispossessed by their own chiefs, the thatch of their bothies often burned over their heads, to make way for the Cheviot sheep which were more profitable than men. They set out across the sea only as a last desperate bid to escape starvation and utter destitution.

The scenes as they left were often harrowing. One account of a sailing from Helmsdale describes how men and women wailed loudly with uncontrolled grief as they went aboard. Some were so overcome with despair they flung themselves to the ground, clinging to the Scottish soil they loved, so that they had to be prised up and carried forcibly to the ship. On board there would be little to comfort them, for the emigrant ships were hell ships in the hands of greedy speculators. Up to 700 men and women and children would be herded into a tiny dark hold originally designed as a tight fit for half as many. Cleanliness and privacy, let alone comfort, were impossible. Here they might spend the next ten or twelve weeks, their little supplies of oatmeal soon exhausted, the water ration undrinkable, the air stinking and disease rampant.

Yet it was these brave, unhappy souls who, as much as the admirals, explorers and entrepreneurs, carried the spirit of Scotland across the sea to help build the new nations—Australia, New Zealand, Canada, the United States—where loyalty to the homeland across the water persisted down generations.

For those who remained, a new chapter in the story of Scotland and the sea was about to open. The Industrial Revolution was spreading to the Lowland firths and little local boatbuilders were giving way to big shipyards. For the next century some of the greatest ships the world has known were to be launched into Scottish waters. In 1869 the loveliest of them all slid down the ways at Scott and Linton's yard at Dumbarton. She was the *Cutty Sark*, in grace and line the culmination of many fast ocean clippers to come from Scottish yards, and certainly the last to survive from that glorious age of sail, preserved today in dry dock at Greenwich.

The London owner, who had chosen a Scottish designer and a Scottish builder, chose a Scottish skipper for her too. This was George Moodie, who learned his business off his native shores and then in the North Sea coastal trade before going into clippers, which needed men with nerves of steel in command. His exploits with the *Cutty Sark*, her great races against the famous Aberdeen ship *Thermopylae*, her bids to break the 63 day record for the Australian run, are sagas in themselves, but for all that, this beautiful ship was obsolescent the day she was launched. In that same year the Suez Canal was opened, resolving beyond any further doubt the commercial superiority of steam over sail. Scottish seamen had already turned their attention to the new age.

William Bell of Helensburgh staked Scotland's claim as the pioneer of steam navigation by building the paddler *Charlotte Dundas* in 1801 but vested interests smothered his plans. There were 11 more years of effort before his *Comet*, complete with piper on the upper deck, steamed down the Clyde to become the true forerunner of all modern ships. Two years later, also down the Clyde, followed William Denny's *Marjorie*, the first steamer ever to cross the English Channel. Scotland's great shipbuilding era had begun, to reach its zenith in the great trans-Atlantic Cunarders, including all three Queens.

Down the ways too slid many a grey dreadnought and, for the bluejackets of two world wars, the seas of Scotland came to mean the often dismal expanse of Loch Ewe, the Moray Firth or Scapa Flow. The arrival of powered battleships and their new weapons had shifted the centre of sea tactics away from the Channel and made it imperative for the Royal Navy to bottle up the North Sea from Scottish bases.

Today Scotland's sea for most people spells mostly pleasure, whether it is holidaying among the Highlands and Islands on a Macbrayne's steamer or sailing their own small craft. The west coast in particular has been a yachtsman's paradise for as long as the more fashionable Solent, as was evident in 1974 when H.M. the Queen reviewed from the Royal Yacht a sail-past of members of the Royal Northern Yacht Club to mark the club's 150th anniversary, a fitting gesture, as Queen Victoria had done just the same on the club's 50th birthday.

Modern boatbuilding methods have happily put sailing within the reach of thousands but half a century ago, when it was still a rich man's sport, people lined the shore to watch the hugely canvassed J class cutters competing in the famous Clyde Fortnight. If they were lucky they might have a distant glimpse of the King in *Brittania,* neck and neck with the German Kaiser's *Meteor.* It was the Kaiser who scoffed "So the King of England has gone boating with his grocer" when Edward the Seventh took as sailing companion the self made man from a Glasgow tenement who had made a fortune selling tea. But the King and the rest of the world knew Tommy Lipton for what he was, a great Scottish sportsman who spent a reputed £2 million between 1899 and 1930 building the five *Shamrocks* with which he tried so desperately hard to bring back to Britain that most elusive sporting trophy in the world, the *America's* Cup. 'The Ould Mug' as Lipton called it was won at Cowes by the visiting New York yacht *America* in 1851 and even now nobody has ever succeeded in winning it back. Nobody has tried harder or come closer than the rags to riches boy from Clydeside.

His spirit lives on in the hundreds of sailing clubs round the Scottish coast today and (although most of the craft are humbler) the tall ship tradition endures in Scotland's own sail training vessel, the 380-ton, three-masted- top-sail schooner *Captain Scott,* run by the Loch Eil Trust to provide adventure holidays for young men between 16 and 21.

Down the years, however, the great majority of Scotsmen have taken to the sea not for adventure but for the basic necessity of a livelihood. A little inshore fishing to supplement the meagre rewards of crofting had always been found wherever boat could be beached or creek afford shelter, but from about 1815 when the herring industry started to develop, the harvest of the sea became a prime factor in the Scottish economy, and remained so for the next hundred years or more. The fleets of drifters and seine

netters in Scottish harbours today, even the big deep water trawlers of Aberdeen, are a pale shadow of the fleets of grandfather's day.

At the height of the herring heyday 800 drifters could be seen leaving Wick on a tide, 400 from Peterhead, 300 from Fraserburgh and so on. The price was often a heavy one. In an August gale in 1848 there were 124 boats along the East Coast lost overnight. More concentrated in its fury was the October hurricane of 1881 which wiped out half the male population of Eyemouth. Of 45 boats from the little Berwickshire port 26 were smashed against the rocks, drowning 189 men, leaving 263 children destitute. Small wonder that such a coast has bred a race of seamen whose endurance, resourcefulness and courage have won them respect in every tough spot on the globe.

As the search for the new harvest under Scotland's sea opens up yet another chapter in the long story, such qualities will still be needed.

Cakes of a Nation/Brenda Sanctuary

Hear, Land o' Cakes and brither Scots . . . (Robert Burns)

No other country has a tradition of home-baking stronger than Scotland's. For centuries, oats have been its basic cereal crop and consequently the mainstay of the Scots diet. As long ago as 1775, Samuel Johnson wrote in his Dictionary of the English Language, "Oats: a grain, which in England is generally given to horses, but in Scotland supports the people".

It has been said that so long as a Scot had oatmeal, water and a flat stone, he could bake himself a cake. In the early days, ovens were not used in Scotland, the common means of baking being the girdle, a thick, flat, round iron plate with a half-hoop handle that hung by a chain over the hearth. Most chains were designed and made by the local blacksmith, thickness indicating the wealth of the owner. The word girdle is also found as "griddle", perhaps deriving from the old French word 'gredil'.

In many poorer homes where the housewife could not afford a girdle, she cooked her bannocks, scones and oatcakes on a flat stone in the hearth. When the cake was half done it was turned with a bannock spade, long-handled and heart-shaped, often made by the blacksmith to an individual design. To give the cake a crusty outside it was propped up in front of the fire on a flat stone, though in the more prosperous households the housewife may have had a wooden or iron bannock toaster. Equally indispensable for making bannocks, oatcakes and porridge was the porridge stick, or spurtle.

Unfortunately it is not always possible to find a girdle but you can always substitute a flat, thick-bottomed iron frying pan, remembering never to wash it. Rub it with salt and kitchen paper instead.

Bannock: a Scottish term that also embraces oatcakes and scones, most likely derived from the Gaelic 'bannach'.

Basically, it means a large cake about the size of a dinner plate, although countless variations exist from region to region. Throughout Scotland bannocks and scones are extremely popular. Whereas the English like bread, the Scots prefer cake, and that in great variety. Bannocks can be based on oatmeal, wheat flour, barley or pease-meal. The Selkirk bannock, a great favourite with Queen Victoria: a flat, thick, fruity, round loaf consisting of dough, sugar, butter and sultanas. Like all sweet bannocks, it is usually eaten sliced with butter. Another traditional bannock (from the Outer Isles) is Aran Isenach or Indian bread: a mixture of flour and finely ground Indian corn or meal, shortened with butter.

It was the custom on Highland quarter days to serve a special Highland Quarter cake; St. Bride's bannock on St. Bride's Day (February 1st or Candlemas Eve, which heralds the Spring); Beltane bannocks or Bonnach Bealltain on May Day. Traditionally a cross was put on the bannock, which the herdsman would throw in pieces over his shoulder, as an offering to such predators as foxes and eagles in the hope that they would leave the sheep unharmed for the following year. Beltain bannocks were often rolled down a hill. If they came to rest unbroken there was supposed to be good fortune to come. Lammas bannocks were baked on August 1st and Hallowmas bannocks on the first of November.

Hallowe'en brings the salt bannock (Bonnach Salainn), eaten in the Highlands to induce dreams foretelling the future. One Shrove Tuesday tradition is the Sauty bannock, a pancake made from oatmeal, eggs and milk. The mixture is dropped, a spoonful at a time, on to a hot, greased girdle. Bree (beef stock) is often used instead of milk. On St. Michael's Eve, September 28th, Scots bake a rich bannock made from flour, currants, caraway seeds, treacle, sugar and milk, the flour being made from the first grain of the year.

Without exception the most important festival in Scotland is Hogmanay. At midnight, "first footers" visit their friends offering drams of whisky, and bannocks baked extra thick for the occasion. Nor have the housewives visited been idle, but more likely busy making Scotch buns or black buns which they offer in return, ensuring good luck for everyone. A Scotch or black bun is a very rich, dark fruit cake encased in pastry. Bun was an old Scots term for a plum cake. On the first Monday after Hogmanay (known as Handsel or Hansel Monday), it is usual to give small presents of money and to receive in return small "Handsel cakes".

There are distinctive bannocks for all Scottish family occasions: cryin' bannocks to celebrate the birth of a baby; christening and teething bannocks with rings cooked in them. These are given to the baby to play with until they are broken, when everyone present, including the baby, gets a small piece. A similar practice exists with the Infar-cake: a rich, crisp oatcake broken over the head of the bride whereat the guests all scramble to pick up fragments, the single person winning the largest being the next to go down the aisle, according to the superstition.

Shortbread: of all the Scottish foods that have achieved popularity abroad, shortbread stands supreme and has even conquered the palate of the "auld enemy" south of the Border. With modern methods, leading manufacturers are able to produce the really genuine buttery shortbread renowned in all parts of the globe, in its instantly recognisable tins or packets distinctively patterned with tartans, heather, Scots pipers, castles or views. At Christmas and Hogmanay great quantities of shortbread are sent abroad from Scotland to friends and relations all over the world. Indeed, in some cases shortbread has taken pride of place on the Scots Hogmanay table, having ousted the traditional Scotch bun.

Shortbread is made with lots of butter, sugar, plain and rice flour, baked in a slow oven to a pale golden brown colour. Some recipes stipulate additions: Edinburgh shortbread has chopped peel or almonds, Bride's Boon from Shetland has caraway seeds and the festive Pitcaithly bannock has almonds and orange peel. There are countless shapes of shortbread. The customary round one with notched edges represents the sun. In Scotland you can buy hand-carved wooden moulds into which the shortbread dough is pressed before being turned out onto a baking sheet for cooking. You can also get Petticoat Tails supposed to be shaped like the hoop petticoats of the Court ladies in the days of the Auld Alliance. There is a theory that Petticoat Tails is a corruption of the French 'Petites Gatelles' or 'Petits Gâteaux'.

Shortbread is delicious eaten on its own. It also appears, however, as an ingredient in many other sweet recipes: crushed shortbread mixed with creamed butter and sugar for a flan pastry case, or mixed with butter and melted chocolate and made into a refrigerated biscuit cake. Another delicious way is to take the shortbread crumbs, soak them in whisky, brandy or sherry and top with fruit and cream. Crumbled shortbread may even be used as a decorative topping for fruit, or in layers with fruit for a Charlotte.

Scone: often mispronouned, the correct pronunciation being 'skoon'. The word suggests many derivations: Sgoon, Gaelic for 'a shapeless mass' or the Middle Dutch, Schoon, meaning 'fine bread'.

Scones can be baked in two ways: on the girdle on top of a stove or in the oven on a baking sheet. They are similar to bannocks but very much smaller and can be cut into quarters (farls) or rounds. Both scones and bannocks should be made with butter milk (or sour milk) and bicarbonate of soda, which produces a softer and moister mixture. Scones can be made either with white or with brown flour, or with barley meal: they can be plain or contain dried fruit or spices. Always, they should be served hot, cut in half and spread with butter. Another favourite on the Scottish tea table is the potato scone, made with mashed potato and cooked on the girdle as is the drop scone. Drop scones are often sold in England as 'Scots pancakes'.

Baps: for breakfast the Scots often have baps: small and flattened white loaves or rolls, traditionally from Aberdeen though now found in many other parts of Scotland and of the world. There are two types of baps: the floury and the buttery.

Gingerbread: gingerbread is a well-loved tea-time cake, ideally moist and black. It can

be made either with flour or with a mixture of oatmeal and flour. In Edinburgh the traditional recipe produces a thick gingerbread full of fruit. The market-places used to sell little gingerbread men, animals or letters of the alphabet. Their shapes used to be moulded by hand but are now more often produced with metal cutters. Until the middle of the nineteenth century it was the custom to coat gingerbread with gold leaf: hence the expression 'to take the gilt off the gingerbread'.

Scots are notably hospitable, and to be invited to tea or to high tea is a great and sometimes awesome experience. The table will probably be piled high with scones, bannocks, shortbread, oatcakes and gingerbread. As Queen Victoria wrote in *More Leaves from the Journal of a Life in the Highlands:* Tuesday, September 16th, 1873: 'While we were stopping to go through one of the locks, a poor woman came and brought us a jug of milk and oatcake which with their usual hospitality the country people constantly offer'.

SCONES

8 oz	250g	2 cup	plain flour
½ tsp	½ tsp	¾ tsp	bicarbonate of soda
½ tsp	½ tsp	¾ tsp	cream of tartar
A pinch of salt			
¼ pt	125ml	¾ cup	buttermilk or sour milk

Baking sheet
Preparation time 10 min
Baking time 10 min

Heat the oven to 425°F, 220°C, mark 7. Grease and flour the baking sheet.

Sift the dry ingredients into a bowl, mix in enough buttermilk or sour milk to make a soft dough. Turn on to a floured board and knead lightly. Roll out to about ½ in, 15 mm, in thickness and cut into rounds about 2 in, 50 mm, across. Place the scones on the prepared baking sheet and bake in a hot oven, 425°F, 220°C, mark 7 for 10 mins.

GINGERBREAD

8 oz	250g	2 cup	plain flour
½ tsp	½ tsp	¾ tsp	bicarbonate of soda
1½ tsp	1½ tsp	2 tsp	ground ginger
1½ tsp	1½ tsp	2 tsp	ground cinnamon
4 oz	100g	½ cup	butter
4 oz	100g	1 cup	soft brown sugar
3 tbsp	50ml	4 tbsp	black treacle
4 tbsp	65ml	⅓ cup	warm milk
1	1	1	egg

Tin 7 in square by 1 in,
175 mm square by 25 mm
Saucepan.
Preparation time 20 min
Baking time 1 to 1½ hours

Heat the oven to 325°F, 170°C, mark 3. Grease and flour the baking tin.

Sift the flour, bicarbonate of soda, ground ginger and cinnamon into a large bowl. Melt the butter, sugar and treacle in a saucepan, cool and stir the milk into the melted butter and pour slowly into the centre of the flour, stirring all the time.

Beat the egg and stir into the flour mixture, beat well and pour into the prepared baking tin. Bake in a moderately low oven, 325°F, 170°C, mark 3 for 1 to 1½ hours. Cool and turn out of the baking tin. Cut into squares.

SELKIRK BANNOCK

2 oz	50g	4 tbsp	butter
2 oz	50g	4 tbsp	lard
½ pt	250ml	1¼ cup	warm milk
½ oz	15g	¾ cake	fresh yeast
½ tsp	½ tsp	¾ tsp	sugar
1 lb	500g	4 cup	plain flour
8 oz	250g	2 cup	sultanas
4 oz	100g	½ cup	sugar

Baking sheet
Preparation time 2 hours
Baking time 1 to 1½ hours

Melt the butter and lard until soft, remove from the heat and add the milk. Cream the yeast with the half teaspoonful of sugar and add to the butter and milk.

Sift the flour into a large bowl, making a well in the centre and pour in the milk, butter and yeast mixture, cover the yeast mixture with the flour from the sides of the bowl. Cover the bowl with a cloth and leave in a warm place for one hour.

Warm the sultanas and sugar. Knead the flour and yeast mixture and add the warmed sultanas and sugar. Knead again and mould into a round, flat bun, place on a greased baking sheet and leave covered with a cloth for a further 40 min.

Remove the cover from the bannock and bake in a moderate oven, 350°F, 180°C, mark 4 for 1 to 1½ hours until it is lightly browned. Test the bannock with a skewer to make sure that it is cooked thoroughly. When cool, serve sliced with butter.

SCOTCH BUN

For the casing
4 oz	100g	$\frac{1}{2}$ cup	butter
8 oz	250g	2 cup	plain flour
$\frac{1}{2}$ tsp	$\frac{1}{2}$ tsp	$\frac{3}{4}$ tsp	baking powder
2 tbsp	25ml	$2\frac{1}{2}$ tbsp	water

For the filling
6 oz	150g	$1\frac{1}{2}$ cup	plain flour
$\frac{1}{2}$ tsp	$\frac{1}{2}$ tsp	$\frac{3}{4}$ tsp	cream of tartar
$\frac{1}{4}$ tsp	$\frac{1}{4}$ tsp	$\frac{1}{2}$ tsp	bicarbonate of soda
1 tsp	1 tsp	$1\frac{1}{4}$ tsp	mixed spice
1 tsp	1 tsp	$1\frac{1}{4}$ tsp	ground cinnamon
1 tsp	1 tsp	$1\frac{1}{4}$ tsp	ground ginger
4 oz	100g	1 cup	Demerara sugar
12 oz	350g	2 cup	raisins
12 oz	350g	3 cup	currants
3 oz	75g	$\frac{2}{3}$ cup	chopped and blanched almonds
4 oz	100g	1 cup	mixed peel
1	1	1	egg
$\frac{1}{4}$ pt	125ml	$\frac{1}{3}$ cup	milk

For the glaze
1	1	1	beaten egg

Cake tin 8 in by 3 in,
225 mm by 75 mm
Preparation time 20 min
Baking time 3 hours

Heat the oven to 350°F, 180°C, mark 4. Grease and flour the cake tin.

For the casing:
Rub the butter into the flour, add the baking powder and mix to a stiff paste with the water. Roll out the pastry on a floured board and line the cake tin, reserving enough pastry to make a lid for the cake.

For the filling:
Sift the flour, cream of tartar, bicarbonate of soda, mixed spice, ground cinnamon and ginger into a bowl. Stir in the Demerara sugar, dried fruit, almonds and mixed peel. Beat the egg and mix into the fruit mixture with the milk. Put the mixture into the pastry casing, cover with the pastry lid, prick with fork and brush with the beaten egg.

Bake in a moderate oven, 350°F, 180°C, mark 4 for 1 hour, then reduce the heat to 300°F, 150°C, mark 2 and cook for a further 2 hours on the lowest shelf. Turn the cake out and serve cold.

Scotch bun will keep for about two weeks in an airtight cake tin.

CRULLAS

4	4	4	eggs
4 oz	100g	$\frac{1}{2}$ cup	butter
4 oz	100g	$\frac{1}{2}$ cup	sugar
$\frac{1}{2}$ tsp	$\frac{1}{2}$ tsp	$\frac{3}{4}$ tsp	bicarbonate of soda
$\frac{1}{2}$ tsp	$\frac{1}{2}$ tsp	$\frac{3}{4}$ tsp	cream of tartar
8 oz	250g	2 cup	plain flour

Deep frying pan with 3 in,
75 mm, of oil
Preparation time 20 min
Cooking time 5 to 8 min

Beat the eggs thoroughly. Cream the butter and sugar together, then add the bicarbonate of soda, cream of tartar and the eggs. Mix well and work in enough flour to make a firm dough.

Put the dough on to a floured board and roll out into an oblong shape. Cut the dough into strips about 4 in by 3 in, 100 mm by 75 mm, then cut each strip into three pieces, leaving one end of the strip uncut. Plait the pieces of dough together, wetting the edges of each piece with water so that they stick firmly together.

Heat the oil and toss the crullas in the hot oil for 5 to 8 min or until they are a light golden brown. Drain the crullas on kitchen paper and serve hot sprinkled with sugar.

When is a nation not a nation? When it is Scotland, perhaps. All good Scots insist that Scotland is a nation, and not simply the most northerly region of the United Kingdom. They have history on their side. Scotland was an ancient and independent kingdom before it joined England under a common monarchy and later under a united Parliament. It has never ceased to be a nation, though it has no government of its own, no legislature, no separate representation on international bodies. It is not, that is to say, a state, but it still retains some of the marks of a nation, for it has its own national church, its separate courts and legal system, and its independent educational set-up. Above all, Scots take it for granted that they have a national identity, that they are different from their English friends, not only in accent and not only in Homeric contests at Wembley and Hampden.

What, then are the outward and visible signs of Scottishness? Outsiders have no difficulty in recognising these. Tartan, the bagpipes, porridge, whisky, the kilt, Highland games, Highland cattle and red deer—Scotland has a superabundance of symbols and features by which it is fixed in the imagination of foreigners. Of course, men wearing the kilt are to be seen in Scotland; a regimental pipe band is a stirring sight; whisky is common enough, if increasingly expensive; and red deer swarm in the remoter glens and hills, as they did when Landseer used to paint them. But these things belong to a romantic and picturesque Scotland, created by Sir Walter Scott and Queen Victoria, who loved Deeside and who gave a boost to tourism, which naturally exploits the colourful aspects of the country. In the workaday world of the ordinary Scot, the romantic heritage fades in the light of common day.

It would be wrong, however, to go to the other extreme, to see Scotland as a grim place defaced by industrial squalor and bad housing, dominated by kill-joy Calvinists, strictly observing the Sabbath, and shutting licensed premises at absurdly early hours. Times have changed, and for the better, in social life, though not all the warts have been removed.

Like Gaul, Scotland is divided into three parts—the Highlands, the Lowlands and the Southern Uplands. As the name implies, the Highlands are mostly mountainous country, separated from the Lowlands by a distinct geological line running from Stonehaven to Dumbarton. Yet there are stretches of low-lying fertile ground around the east coast of the Highland region where farming is efficiently pursued. Livestock rearing is the chief activity of Scottish farmers, who do a brisk export trade in cattle and sheep. Aberdeen-Angus beef, for instance, has a prime reputation. Sheep are pastured on the hills and in the glens of the Highlands, and there are large flocks on the grassy mountains of the Southern Uplands, where the abundance of wool has given rise to the textile industries of Hawick, Selkirk and other Border towns.

Wheat is grown on the rich soil of the Lothians, but oats and barley are much more common crops, the latter being used in making whisky. In Lanarkshire market gardening, especially the growing of tomatoes, is well established and fruit for canning, principally raspberries, is a valuable Perthshire crop. Scottish farming has a considerable variety of produce; it is up to date in machinery and techniques, and it is backed by an extensive system of agricultural research and education. In contrast with mechanised farming, thousands of crofts (small farms) survive in the Highlands and islands; they barely provide subsistence, the crofters usually having some other occupation, such as fishing or weaving, for the land is too meagre to permit large-scale farming.

Though the largest in area, the Highland region is the most thinly populated. Much of it comprises moors and mountains, too barren and high lying to nourish anything but grouse and red deer, which provide sport for the affluent. It is, however, a land of scenic splendour, spectacularly rocky and mountainous. Even in the austere expanses of the far North-West, it possesses a desolate beauty. Naturally, it has become increasingly popular with tourists, so the narrow roads are gradually being improved. For hill-walkers and anglers the Highlands are a happy hunting-ground, whilst in the inland and sea lochs there is plenty of scope for sailing, which is especially popular in the Firth of Clyde. Fishing, for sport or as an industry, is by no means confined to the Highlands, though it is a common means of livelihood in the islands, and in the small towns of the west coast. Aberdeen is the busiest fishing port in Scotland; its trawlers bring in from Icelandic and more distant waters catches which are speedily dispatched to Billingsgate in London.

Farming, fishing and forestry are carried on throughout Scotland, but in the Highlands the work of the Forestry Commission is particularly valuable in making use of inferior land. Some think large forests of conifers make the landscape monotonous, that more planting of hardwoods would be desirable, but the Forestry Commission are obliged to put commercial before aesthetic considerations. Whisky is a product often associated with the Highlands, but distilleries and bonded warehouses are spread widely over Scotland, though the greatest concentration is to be found in Speyside and Banffshire. It is an industry that does not provide a great deal of employment, but it is an inexhaustible source of revenue for the Exchequer, one of Britain's most profitable exports, and an especially valuable dollar-earner. Scotland makes a substantial contribution to Britain's export trade, with high quality textiles from the Border towns, Harris tweed from the Hebrides, its Clyde-built ships, as well as its whisky, for which world demand remains insatiable.

The central part of Scotland is the Lowlands. In comparison with the Highlands and the Southern Uplands it may justly be called low, but it contains several ranges of hills rising to some 2,000 feet. It is the heartland of the country, for it includes three cities, most of the large burghs (boroughs), about three-quarters of the population and nearly all the manufacturing industry. Here were located the coal and iron deposits, the exploitation of which last century made Scotland a great centre of shipbuilding, steel-making and engineering. It had the materials for building ships, the banks of the Clyde were natural sites for shipyards, and Clydeside workers developed a high tradition of skill in engineering. The iron reserves are now exhausted: coal output has shrunk far below the zenith reached about 1914; and shipbuilding has consequently declined in terms of tonnage and men employed. With imported iron ore the Scottish steelworks are still a major industry, and so is shipbuilding, the Scott-Lithgow works on the lower reaches of the Clyde being highly efficient and profitable. But the long decline of the heavy industries, once the basis of Scotland's prosperity, was a painful experience. The country failed, perhaps because too much capital and skill had been invested in shipbuilding and marine engineering, to make a timely entry into the manufacture of new, mass-produced goods, such as cars, radios and electrical appliances.

The depression of the 1930s hit Scotland with particular severity; its unemployment and emigration figures were, and still are, higher than those of most regions of England. Yet since the war there has been a sustained effort to adjust to changed industrial demands. Government policies giving special incentives to industrialists to open factories in areas of high unemployment benefited Scotland, along with the efforts of native bodies like the Scottish Council to widen the range of industries. The Scottish economy was reinforced by the arrival of a considerable number of American firms whose technological experience had a stimulating effect. Now dependence on heavy industries has greatly diminished. Clocks and watches, office equipment, earth-moving machinery and computers are among the goods produced on a large scale in Scotland, which has also acquired a useful stake in the electronics industry. It gained too, through Government persuasion or pressure on motor manufacturers, two big plants for the assembly of cars and commercial vehicles. The troubles which beset the automobile everywhere have not been lacking in Scotland, and the ventures have not been altogether profitable, as the Scottish sector is not quite large enough to attract the makers of components who supply the Midlands works, so that transport costs are a burden.

Remarkable headway has been made in the task of clearing away scars left on the landscape by the older enterprises. Coal and shale bings, drab rows of single-storey houses in mining villages, and waste lands where factories once stood were the legacy of the industrial revolution. With Government grants grimy features have been removed and the environment made more attractive for modern industry. New towns, like East Kilbride and Cumbernauld, have proved a magnet for industrialists and housed some of Glasgow's surplus population, giving the city more space to develop within its own boundaries. Glasgow's renewal is symbolic of the change that is taking place in Scotland. The Gorbals and other notorious slums are being swept away; motorways are being driven through the city; and, though multi-storey flats and high office blocks are not everybody's idea of civic amenity, there is no doubt that the new Glasgow which is rising will be a better place to live in than was the old warren of tenements and factory chimneys. Not that Glasgow was ever as bad as realist novelists made it appear. It always had a warm social life, amid sporadic violence, and its proximity to fine scenery, notably Loch Lomond, and its comfortable suburbs, offset its rather besmirched appearance.

Environmental improvement has been materially boosted by Scotland's continuing success in attracting a wide variety of lighter industries to diversify and to stabilize employment. However, until recently those engaged in promoting new growth in the Scottish economy had an uphill fight. In spite of the regional policies of successive Governments, the prospects of success were doubtful; it seemed a case of running hard to stay in the same spot.

Then the discovery of North Sea oil introduced a new dimension. Its importance was not realised at the outset, but now there is no danger of underestimating its far-reaching consequences. Estimates of the extent of the oil deposits, of their value, of their contribution to the revenue and so on are necessarily provisional, for there is much prospecting to be done yet and the costs of getting oil ashore are escalating fast, as are those of other industrial operations. Still, by 1980 the flow of North Sea oil should be sufficient to provide for Britain's own requirements and leave a substantial margin for export. It is the security against which British Governments are borrowing to close the gap between now and the future years of oil in plenty. The Government has an obvious interest in speeding up the production of North Sea oil, both in order to repay international debts and to tap a rich source of revenue. But the work in the North Sea is difficult and hazardous; the technical problems are formidable; and the oil companies naturally want an adequate return on their capital. The Government propose to levy royalties, corporation tax and petroleum revenue tax on the oil companies and to take a 51% holding in the oilfields. There is the usual conflict between the oil operators and the Governments of the oil-producing countries about the division of the spoils. Such disputes will presumably be settled by satisfactory compromise. Politics apart, the proven oil reserves are large enough to ensure that Scotland will be an oil producer on the scale of Venezuela and Libya.

So far oilfields have been proved about 100 miles off Aberdeen and near the Shetland islands. Oil rigs engaged in the exploration have mostly been built abroad, and the prospecting directed by Americans, as British firms lacked experience of drilling for oil under the sea bed. But oil exploitation has already brought great benefit to Scotland and promises to create a veritable boom. Aberdeen has become the centre of oil operations, a port for servicing rigs at sea, and the headquarters of oil companies and of other firms supplying them with materials. Other ports on the east coast, like Dundee, are also providing facilities for the oil rigs and their suppliers. Meanwhile, preparations are going on for bringing the oil ashore. Oil production platforms, enormous structures of steel or concrete, are being built at Invergordon and Ardersier around the Moray Firth and at Ardyne point on the Clyde. Pipe-lines are being laid to the Aberdeenshire coast, and there will be a vast terminal for oil tankers and storage at Sullom Voe in Shetland. Deep water is needed for the building of concrete production platforms, and it happens that the best sites are to be found around the west coast, some unfortunately in places of outstanding scenic appeal. Already there have been fierce battles between conservationists and those who would sacrifice the peace and grandeur of Highland lochs in order to tap the oil reserves as quickly as possible.

Oil is not an unmixed blessing, but clearly it will give a tremendous boost to Scottish industry, to steelmakers and to engineering firms able to cater for its wide range of equipment. It will also speed up the improvement of roads, air services, housing, schools and other facilities needed by the new or enlarged communities employed in building platforms or constructing terminals to cope with the oil flow. For its small population (just over five million) Scotland has a good stock of roads. They have been improved, though slowly, and the building of two large road bridges over the Forth and the Tay has provided quick passage in place of weary waits for ferries. The oil boom will accelerate work on the widening of the Perth – Inverness road, which is hopelessly inadequate for its present volume of traffic.

Discovery of a new and rich natural resource may revolutionise the Scottish economy. It has already had an explosive effect on Scottish politics. For most of the nineteenth century Scotland was solidly Liberal, but as the Liberal party split and declined,the Labour party extended its representation and the Conservatives also enlarged their stake. In 1955 the Conservatives held half the country's 71 seats, but they have gradually lost ground, until at the last election (October, 1974) they

were reduced to 16 seats. Labour's score was 41 seats, but the most sensational feature of the election was the advance of the Scottish National Party. They increased their aggregate vote to more than 800,000, much greater than that of the Conservatives, but, owing to the eccentricities of the British electoral system, they emerged with only 11 MPs.

The prospect of an oil bonanza and the progress of the SNP are closely connected. Oil found in Scottish waters, the party argue, should be the property of the Scottish people who, if they were independent, could profit from it as Norway is doing. Still, it would be unfair and misleading to imply that Scottish nationalism and the growing support for it spring solely from desire to enjoy all the wealth of the North Sea. The movement was in existence before oil was dreamed of, and the discovery of a new source of riches removed an objection which used to be regarded as fatal to claims for self-government, namely that Scotland could not exist, or rather could not maintain its living standards, without subsidies from Westminster. This assumption was often challenged, and never proved, but it was widely accepted and had been cited by Labour as a conclusive reason for rejecting Home Rule.

Scotland does possess a certain degree of Home Rule in the administrative field. In the 1930s the administration of Scottish affairs moved from London to Edinburgh, where St Andrew's House is the modest counterpart of Whitehall. The Scottish Office comprises five Departments, dealing with an immense range of business, such as housing, health, agriculture, planning, local government, and education. It is responsible to the Secretary of State for Scotland, always a member of the Cabinet, who is helped by a Minister of State and two or three junior Ministers. In spite of this administrative devolution, Nationalists complain that all important decisions are still made in London, and that vital powers concerning industrial development are exercised in Scotland by UK Ministries.

The SNP's take-off should be seen against a background of gradual devolution, of which people outside Scotland are seldom aware. Now all the Scottish parties are devolutionists. Labour are committed to setting up an elected legislature in Scotland to deal with the functions already under the Secretary of State's control, but it is not known what powers it will have in economic and financial affairs. After their setback in the election the Conservatives have raised their bid to rival that of Labour. Liberals who have three seats in Scotland, stand for a federal system for the UK. The SNP's policy of independence is clear-cut, but it is fair to say that they have no racial prejudice and no desire to set up trade barriers between Scotland and England. They are supported by many who would settle for less than independence, but who see the SNP as the strongest force for securing Scottish control of domestic affairs. There is no denying that the success of the SNP has speedily converted Labour to the necessity of conceding some political devolution.

As a nation, Scots are not unrelievedly dour, hard-headed, totally dedicated to making money. They have not the artistic traditions of some of the small European nations, like Austria, but the cultural scene is by no means barren. Apart from Scott and Burns, Scottish writers are little known abroad, but today there are poets and novelists of merit; the annual exhibitions of the Royal Scottish Academy reach praiseworthy standards of painting and sculpture; and there are some composers of promise. Edinburgh's International Festival of the Arts is about the largest and most varied of the numerous festivals held in Europe. It used to be said that it was all imported and that it did nothing to stimulate the arts in Scotland itself. This is no longer true, for Scottish Opera is well established and known outside its own country. Like the Scottish National Ballet, it draws on outside talent, but it is gratifying that these ventures have taken root in a nation with a rather thin tradition in the theatrical arts. The Scottish National Orchestra lives up to its title, and with repertory theatres, art galleries and museums Scotland is well furnished.

Art has often been the handmaiden of religion. In Scotland it was commonly held that the Presbyterian faith, derived from Calvinism, was hostile to the arts. This was debatable, but it is certainly not true now. The Church of Scotland, the national church, with a membership of more than a million, is established, but (unlike the Church of England) it is free from state intervention in appointments, worship or doctrine. The numerical strength of the Roman Catholic Church in Scotland is not much less than that of the national church, but it is concentrated in the central region, most of its members being descended from Irish immigrants. Inter-church relations are very amicable; the ecumenical movement has softened prejudices; and Roman Catholic schools are on equal terms with those of the state, which is not the case in England and Northern Ireland.

Educationally Scotland is well equipped to benefit from the oil revolution. She produces every year more graduates in science, engineering and technology than she can employ, and many of them have to emigrate. Some of the universities have introduced courses for training oil technologists and are doing research in off-shore engineering. There are eight universities in Scotland, four of them ancient foundations, the others products of the post-war expansion of higher education. Strathclyde and Heriot-Watt universities, though recently upgraded, were originally colleges of technology and have retained that bias. Edinburgh University has a famous Medical School; Glasgow University is distinguished for science and engineering; St Andrews, the oldest of them all, has more of the atmosphere of Oxbridge. The Scottish universities are only partly residential; they prefer lecturing to the tutorial system; and generally they have been efficient institutions for training lawyers, clergymen, accountants and doctors.

On the lower level, the school system has striking differences from that of England. Public schools are few, mostly exotic transplants. There are fee-paying schools, with high reputations, in Edinburgh and Glasgow. The overwhelming majority of pupils, however, go to state schools, and even before the days of Government grants for students it was possible for poor children to get to the top of the educational ladder. Scottish schools suffer now from the general malaise in education, the slackening of discipline, the uncertainty of aims, shortage and discontent of teachers, most of whom are well qualified.

Nevertheless, the general level of public concern for educational standards is as high in Scotland now as it always has been, and such concern is the hallmark of a progressive nation. Educational, cultural and economic progress all ultimately depend on a free and continuous interchange of ideas between nations, so perhaps it is not altogether surprising that one of the most successful Scottish business enterprises of recent years is an airline, ferrying an ever-growing stream of goods and people between Scotland and the outside world.

Glasgow-born Adam Thomson was a founder of the enterprise, which began operating charter flights on a modest scale in 1961, using leased aircraft. Now chairman and chief executive of British Caledonian Airways, he has seen the company grow larger than two-thirds of the world's scheduled airlines, numbering many Scottish banks, insurance companies and investment trusts amongst its financial backers.

Nine clan chieftains have given BCAL permission to use their clan tartans for the kilted uniforms worn by air hostesses. These and the lion rampant emblems on tail fins and the atmosphere engendered of traditional Scottish hospitality give the airline a strongly Scottish character, which does not prevent it from being strongly British, as the official flag-carrier on many major international routes: for example, those serving many countries of West Africa, South America, Tripoli (Libya), Genoa (Italy) and the Canary Islands. Altogether over $2\frac{1}{2}$ million passengers were carried in 1973, and 32 thousand tons of freight, but British Caledonian Airways' importance to the Scottish and British economies can perhaps best be gauged from its foreign earnings, almost £90 million to date.

Scotch whisky is the native and inimitable spirit of Scotland born of the four elements of that land—its earth, air, fire and water—by the creative genius of that proud, independent, hard-working folk. Not the alchemist's den nor the laboratory of the philosopher seeking the elixir of life was the scene of its birth, but the farm or field, bothy or castle. It began as a creature of everyday life in its rural environment, and now like the Scots themselves is to be found around the world, again like the Scots, supreme, as the world's premier potable spirit.

In 1973, the latest full year to hand at writing, its exports amounted to 78,450,000 proof gallons worth £259,985,000, increases of 14 per cent. in both volume and value compared with the previous year, and home consumption shot up 21.96 per cent. to over 15,348,000 gallons. As Mr George Grant, president of The Malt Distillers' Association of Scotland said at their centenary banquet in October, 1974: 'What was at its outset a family industry is now a national industry of the greatest importance to the nation's economy with its massive export market.' In the first half of 1974, again, exports were up 21 per cent. in volume to 42,283,000 gallons and 29 per cent. in value to over £148,885,000. This

Scotland Distilled/Ross Wilson

from, by birth, a family industry! There lies the romance, the mystery, the success of Scotch whisky.

But born a family cottage industry, no note was made of its inception. As the Middle Ages drew to their close, the learned called it *aqua vitae*, the ordinary folk, *uisge beatha*, both meaning the same thing—water of life. Today, we have contracted that Gaelic name to—whisky.

Almost forebodingly, the Scottish Exchequer Rolls of 1494 contain its first written record, providing 'eight bolls of malt to Friar John Cor wherewith to make aqua vitae'. A boll was ten stones. That is, before the end of the 15th century Scotch whisky, however named, was receiving official recognition, so long had it been in existence.

It was accepted, too, at the royal table: the accounts of the Lord High Treasurer of Scotland record a payment of 'ix shillings' to the 'barbour' who brought aqua vitae to the King in Dundee. Its medicinal value was early spotted: in 1505 the City of Edinburgh granted a monopoly of making it to the Guild of Surgeon Barbers. In September of the following year twice was payment made for supplying the King with it in Inverness.

This royal acclaim and acceptance has persisted through the centuries, the most recent occasion being when the Duke of Edinburgh proposed the health of The Malt Distillers' Association of Scotland in October 1974 at their centenary banquet at Aviemore in Inverness-shire.

Monopolies are repugnant to most people, and it comes as no surprise that a hardy Highland woman challenged that of the Edinburgh Surgeon Barbers some 50 years after its original grant. Caught out, the Edinburgh Bailies bade her 'to desist and ceis from making aqua vitae within the burgh in the time coming' unless she had the barbers' permission to do so. Uisge beatha, or aqua vitae, or whisky, flows henceforth in a constant stream through the history of Scotland. We cannot list every occurrence, but this passage from Holinshed's *Chronicles,* published in 1577 and used by Shakespeare in writing *Macbeth* cries out for quotation: 'Beying moderatelie taken, it sloweth age; it strengtheneth youthe; it helpeth digestion; it cutteth fleume; it abandoneth melancholie; it relisheth the harte; it lighteneth the mynde; it quickeneth the spirites ... trulie it is a soueraigne liquor.'

For centuries, then, whisky-making was simply a sideline to farming. One example must suffice. In January, 1655, Robert Haig, tenant of Throsk Farm in St. Ninian's parish near Stirling was charged before the Parish Session with distilling on the Sabbath, but only 'rebuked' when it was found that the servant lass had simply finished distilling some left-over material.

A typical incident of farm life. For whisky was embedded deep in daily life. One constant prayer: 'Heaven preserve us from the illness whisky will not cure.' It played its part in every one of the climacterics of life: birth, mating and death. To take but one instance: William Grant of Rothiemurchus was born in 1798 and his nurse gave him a spoonful of gin even before she washed him. Most unorthodox: she should have given him a small spoonful of earth and the whisky drawn from it. Always, everywhere, the baby's visitors were offered whisky, cheese and shortbread.

On marriage, especially in the Hebrides, the newly-weds were expected to sit up in bed to receive their guests; whisky was passed around, and to end the proceedings one of the party threw two glassfuls of it in the faces of the bride and groom. Something the same almost happened to Shelley and his bride Harriet Westbrook in Edinburgh after their marriage. The intruding landlord of the hotel was forced out by an irate Shelley armed with pistols.

For very nearly ninety years during the 18th century the Forbeses of Culloden could distil their whisky free of duty from the grain grown on their own fertile lands, as a result of a settlement made by the Scots Parliament in 1695 and a claim by Duncan Forbes whose large estate had been totally devastated by the Jacobites six years earlier and, in his own words, "suffered the loss of his brewery and aqua vitae by fire in his absence".

As to that final arbiter, death, Smollett gives us this report in his *Humphry Clinker*: 'Yesterday we were invited to the funeral of an old lady and found ourselves in the midst of fifty people, who were regaled with a sumptuous feast. In short, this meeting had all the air of a grand festival; and the guests did such honour to the entertainment, that many of them could not stand when we were reminded of the business on which we had met ... We returned to the castle, resumed the bottle, and by midnight there was not a sober person in the family, the females excepted ... Our entertainer seemed to think it a disparagement to his family that not above an hundred gallons of whisky had been drunk upon such a solemn occasion.'

So flowed Scotch through every phase of the Scotsman's life: from the cradle to the grave, from first thing in the morning to the last thing at night. And on all occasions between.

But the taxman's doom was waiting in the wings. Pitt the Younger assumed power in England and began, in 1784, a 'reform' of distillery laws, a reform that lasted 40 years. Rates of tax on spirit and distiller varied incessantly; Scotland was divided and sub-divided and re-formed again and again. One prolonged—and ineffective—method of taxing the distiller and his product, for example, was to measure (gauge) the still, assess its spirit production and tax it accordingly. The result was a race between the taxman and the distiller: as the distiller made more and more whisky from the same sized still, so that duty rate was increased. One important change was that distillers altered the shape of their stills from tall and narrow to broad-based and low so as to distil more rapidly. The shape has remained to this day.

One of the most important results of this English interference with Scottish whisky making was the golden age of illicit distillers, the smugglers, particularly in the Highlands and Islands of the land. For the smugglers became the true inheritors, guardians and transmitters of the ancient Scottish traditions of distilling the water of life. By instinct and experience they chose the best sites for their operations and today the best malt whisky distilleries are either on the same sites or in the same regions as favoured by those true pioneers of Scotch. Their ruses to escape detection are unnumerable and as fascinating as true. They needed remote spots with an unpolluted air, ample soft, fresh water, plenty of peat and barley to hand—the four prime elements of Scotland. Two brief examples must suffice. At Lagavulin, on the south-east tip of the Isle of Islay, were no less than ten smugglers' bothies: legal today, the distillery makes upward of 750,000 gallons of malt whisky a year. Indeed, Islay smuggling was so successful it was a major occupation of the island and today eight major distilleries continue the trend.

On the other side of Scotland, the most prolific region for the smugglers—and now the most prolific for malt whisky—in the north-east of Scotland, there were no fewer than 200 smugglers in the glen of the Livet, a tributary of the Spey river. One of them, a farmer by the name of George Smith, used to make 3,000 gallons a year. When the distillery laws were rationalized in 1823 he decided to become a legal distiller—the first under the new system—he made 10,000 gallons in his first legal year, and such was and is the fame of The Glenlivet whisky that today the same—though greatly enlarged—distillery makes 1,300,000 gallons a year. So irate were his fellow smugglers at his 'treachery' that for years he went armed, but so famous was his whisky that George IV demanded Glenlivet (illegal) whisky on his 1822 visit to Edinburgh, the first Hanoverian king to visit Scotland.

'The whole country went mad,' wrote Elizabeth Grant of Rothiemurchus. 'Lord Conyngham, the Chamberlain, was looking everywhere for pure Glenlivet whisky; the King drank nothing else. It was not to be had out of the Highlands. My father sent word to me . . . to empty my pet bin, where was whisky long in wood, long in uncorked bottles, mild as milk, and the true contraband gout in it . . . It made our fortune afterwards. . . '

That 1823 reform of the distillery and whisky tax laws marks the beginning of the modern age of Scotch, though it was to take another 50 years before Scotch began its conquest of the English market, from where it set out on its world victories.

Smugglers turned legal, old distilleries were enlarged, new ones built, such as that erected by William Grant and his sons at a cost of under £120—the daughters cut the peat—capable of making about 5,000 gallons a year when it came on stream on Christmas Day, 1887. Enlarged, today it makes 2.5m. gallons a year or more. But located in the glen of the Fiddich, another tributary of the Spey, from which it takes its name of Glenfiddich, it still takes its vital water from the spring of Robbie Dubh. Made with any other water it would cease to be the Glenfiddich malt whisky known everywhere, and, as we shall now see, the same is true of all malt whisky distilleries.

For malt whisky made by the ancient traditional craft, however much modern mechanical aids have been called into play, is the root and stem of the whole Scotch Whisky industry, the central core from which is has grown and branched until today, despite vicissitudes of every kind, it is the premier potable spirit of the world. It is time to turn to look more closely into the craft.

Today, the strict quality control at every distillery demands the most exact measurement, testing and phasing at every stage of the whole process. Nothing is haphazard. The distillery is either sited close to its water supply, generally a spring, or the chosen water is brought miles from an almost inaccessible spot. A very serious argument prevails at this point: which is to be preferred?—Water coming off red granite and passing through peat, or water from peat that has flowed over red granite?

Only carefully tested and selected barley is received in, and once in the plant is left to rest under carefully controlled conditions of storage. Cleansed, it passes, weighed, to be soaked in a steep containing the distillery's chosen water, a matter of only a few days in which the water is changed from time to time. When judged correct, the wet barley is spread out on the malting floor of stone or concrete to begin its controlled germination. That is, it is allowed to begin sprouting so that Nature's own processes of conversion may take control. Day and night the sprouting barley is turned by maltmen using wooden shovels, or skips, allowing the growing barley to breathe and preventing its rootlets becoming a tangled mass. Within the barley, enzymes are busily at work converting its starch into saccharine matter which would normally feed the growing plant. When the barley's shoot, or acrospire, is about two-thirds the length of the grain, the maltman knows it is time to call a halt.

He does it with the aid of that primitive fuel of the Highlands, peat, used for firing for long ages before coal. The green malt, as it is now termed, though there is nothing green about it, is transported to that distinguished feature of every malt distillery, the peat-fired kiln crowned with a pagoda. There the green malt is spread on a mesh metal floor and while the peat burns merrily away sending its smoke with its precious odour through the malt 20 or so feet above, the malt is turned so that the heat and the peat reek may be spread evenly through the malt.

So the elements of earth and fire combine to stop the germination without destroying the life-principle while giving to the malt that savour that is essentially and forever Scotland. Smell, taste, your next Scotch carefully and slowly; enjoy the peat reek, the odour of Scotland, brought to your hand.

Many distillers have today given up malting for themselves on a floor. Some use large rotating drums where air is carefully blown through the wet barley, some use large Saladin concrete 'boxes' where ploughs turn the barley, some have it done for them at central plants. But always it is done carefully with just the right peat reek.

After its ordeal by fire, the malt is carefully stripped of its rootlets, weighed and subjected to the hot water treatment. This is where the distinctive character of the distiller's chosen water influences the character and quality of the whisky. Ground into fragments the malt is mashed in a metal tun with hot water, the enzymes resume their conversion activities and the revolving, mashing arms in the tun keep them at peak action also helping the water to dissolve the sugary matter in the malt. The tun is drained and the liquid—worts—cooled ready for fermenting. Again the malt is mashed, with even hotter water, the draining repeated and the worts sent cooled for fermenting. Twice more, each time with hotter and hotter water, the malt is mashed, but these weak worts are held over to become the first hot waters of the next mashing.

Cooled to the exactly right temperature, the worts are pumped to large fermenting backs, cylindrical vessels of larch, oak or stainless steel, there to be torn apart by carefully selected and tested yeasts. The husks left behind in the mash tun go to provide cattle food, but the worts undergo such a savage attack by the yeast that switchers are provided to check back the fiercely bubbling worts. Carbon dioxide is flung off into the air and what is left behind is a sort of weak beer, alcohol with the Scottish character of its origin and ordeals embedded deep within it. Rest reigns in the fermenting tun as the converted worts, now named wash in view of its changed internal structure, settles for its next ordeal—by fire.

This is a double ordeal; twice must it be subjected to this distilling torment, which separates out the real, essential character of Scotland in concentrated form. The stills in which this operation takes place have retained their traditional form and resemble large copper onions. The heat may be provided in the form of a coal or oil fire, or it may be by means of steam coils within the still itself. But what the heat does is to cause the alcohol in the mixture—for that is what wash is essentially—to vapourize before most of the water that imprisons it. As the vapours come over the head of the still they are shocked back to liquid form by the impact of cold water and pass under the name of low wines to their own receiver. This is but a rough and ready separation of spirit and water, but all that is Scottish, all that is spirit, is kept close. What remains in the still, the pot ale, is now generally concentrated to become cattle-food.

The low wines then undergo their ordeal by fire, a more slow and careful process in which the first runnings off the still, foreshots, are put aside as not worthy to become Scotch whisky. The middle cuts, the heart of the matter, alone come up to the distiller's standards as new-born whisky and go to their own receiver. The last runnings join the foreshots to be redistilled in the next low wines, and so carry on some continuity of character at the distillery.

There is the spirit of Scotland brought to liquid form; there is the summary, the epitome of a land and people. But, an embodiment that must then undergo a baptismal dilution: it is at once reduced in alcoholic strength with some of the water from which it was born to what the Scotch distiller knows is the right strength to ensure perfect ageing.

The new-born Scotch is like a raw, hot-headed youngster who must mature, grow mellow and gracious.

This is done by imprisoning him in oaken casks locked—the Queen's official has a key to partner the distiller's—in impregnable warehouses on the Scottish hills, in the Scottish glens. There only the pure air of the Scottish countryside is allowed to visit him in his confinement, bearing away all those roughnesses of character he may have acquired in his ordeals by grinding, by fire and hot water. Tamed after years upon years of

imprisonment, he emerges as the gracious Scottish gentleman who has won the hearts and loyalty of millions around the world.

Today whisky may also be made in another fashion by a 'modern' patent still—it was patented in 1831!—and together the two are blended to form the more usual Scotches acclaimed around the world. But the root and stem of it all is the whisky, the water of life, made in the traditional pot still.

Scotch whisky has today ascended the scale from being a cottage industry, a sideline to farming, to that of an industry of national importance and international significance, but still the words of C. E. Montague echo across the mountains and glens of Scotland as around the world:

'What sort of hivven's delight is this you've invented for all souls in glory?'

For a keen angler it is a pleasure to fish on almost any stream, but to fish on the River Spey is a double blessing. For this river is unique in the pleasures it so amply dispenses. From its sources—the ice-cool springs among the Grampian snows and granite rocks—through its headlong course to the Moray Firth, the Spey has a profound influence, not only on the angler who is fortunate enough to cast a line on its reaches, but also on the different "races" who inhabit the Spey Valley.

The climate in the lower valley is dry and temperate. Evidence of early habitation (by Neolithic man as far back as 3500 BC) indicates that the land and its salubrious climate were appreciated in those far-off days. The Vikings pulled their longboats into the mouth of the Spey, liked what they saw and stayed. To this day there is a striking contrast between the fair-complexioned, lightly-freckled, sandy-haired people predominant near the coastal area and the dark-haired, short, square-set highlanders of the hills and glens up river in the hinterland.

Spey and its tributaries afford pleasure, employment (and considerable wealth) to many in the fine malt whiskies which the world has come to appreciate. But for me, the true, distinctive character of the river lies in the wealth of its game angling. This river is unsurpassed in the excellence of its fishing: mile upon mile of salmon pools, mysterious deeps to hold the lethargic spring salmon, and effervescent rushes and tumbling cascades for the summer fish.

Here is the fastest-flowing river in Britain; powerful, with broad rapids and pools changing from rushing white water at the throat to turbulent, swirling eddies in the middle and to fast, smooth-gliding streams in the tail: ideal for sea trout and salmon. In the springtime when the melting Grampian snows bring low water temperatures, the

Lure of the Spey / Alan S. Paterson

salmon lie deep in sluggish water and await more propitious conditions for their upstream migration. The generous Spey provides salmon lies for every season.

How the names of the pools conjure up past exploits and associations, in many instances aptly descriptive: Broom Isle, The Dykes, The Slabs, Gean Trees, Blue Stone, Twa Stanes, The Twenty Pound, The Grilse Pool, The Birks, Cumberland's Ford—these all tell their own story and it is a poor man who does not instantly recognise the happy associations of the Fiddich and the Livet in the vital rôles they play in the making of Speyside malt whisky.

In this strong, swift river a style of fly fishing has evolved to match the water conditions. Traditionally, a spliced greenheart rod fifteen feet or more long, with a sweet, supple action extending all the way into the butt was used with magical effect to roll-cast a fly across as much as forty yards. To see an expert perform this roll-cast, delicately placing a fly, is a superb sight. Nowadays glass fibre and split cane have replaced greenheart, but the Spey cast has stood the test of time and is still a most effective and graceful method of deploying a fly on fast-flowing water, especially where there are obstructions which prevent conventional overhead casting. One of the finest exponents of Spey casting I know is over ninety years old. Even in mid-February last season, whilst lesser mortals were spinning with Devon minnows for spring salmon, George was able to demonstrate the effectiveness of a large fly fished slow and deep on a well-thrown sinking line.

Fly fishing is still the most successful and pleasurable method of catching Spey salmon, especially after the water temperature has risen in the late spring sunshine. Many of the beautiful salmon fly patterns in vogue in the early part of the century, using the brilliant exotic plumage of the toucan, the golden pheasant, the jungle cock, the ostrich, the Indian crow and the macaw, meticulously dressed with composite wings, toppings and even horns, have now been supplanted by less complicated styles of tube flies, hair flies and even less brilliant versions. I am sure that many patterns are designed as much to catch the anglers' fancy as the fishes'. Nonetheless our vocabulary and our catches would be much poorer without such names as Lady Caroline, Jeannie, the Shrimp Fly, Logie, Silver Wilkinson, Hairy Mary, Jock Scott, Munro Killer, Stoat's Tail. These patterns and many variants are used with great effect throughout the Spey, especially from April onwards, as low water flies, sparingly dressed and on needlesharp hooks fished on a floating line.

Spring fishing until April is conditioned by the low water temperatures from the melting Grampian snows. At these temperatures the fish are lethargic and lie deep. The most effective way of tempting the silver beauties with a lure is by spinning. Devon minnows (often of gaudy colours) up to three inches long account for most of the early springers. Anticipation of a duel with some fat, deep-shouldered specimen certainly helps to make the cold winter months of the close season more tolerable. Spring for the salmon fisher comes betimes, early in February. Invariably the lower beats around Gordon Castle, Delfur and Rothes are well stocked with fresh salmon and, in the recent series of mild winters, the early spring run has forged upstream as far as Ballindalloch to the River Avon and beyond. Angling in these early months can be a rewarding if cold sport and one is often glad of that other product of the Spey Valley to bring back the circulation to numb limbs as well as to toast the first fish of the year.

For me, the greatest pleasures of fishing on the Spey derive not from any spectacular feats of angling prowess, but from man's close communion with nature. The fish I catch will be unlikely to feature in record books, but the fond recollection of relatively minor incidents on my fishing trips will always create within me a warm glow. It is hard to describe the deep satisfaction I had from fishing one June night for sea trout, on Upper Aultdearg some years ago. Midsummer was not far off and the sun had sunk, leaving a pale lemon glow in the North-Western sky which moved slowly round to the North-East. Night in June in these latitudes is merely a short period of half-light. The river was low and the air balmy, and I was completely alone with the Spey and its inhabitants, the bats, the owls, the peewits, the oyster-catchers, and of course the fish. Sea trout were running and three tide-fresh fish from $1\frac{3}{4}$ to $3\frac{1}{4}$ lb had accepted my home-made Greenwell's Glory. The recollection of catching these, the sudden tugs from the dark waters and the rush and flurry of the surprised fish, darting and leaping half-seen in the summer dimness are only part of the memory. The scents of the lush, early summer growth, the grey-black silhouettes of the hills, the sound of owls calling and the splashing of the Spey blended into a complete experience which appealed to all the senses. I fished from only ten in the evening till two in the morning, but by the time I left I had seen roe deer swim the river, watched a sunset, a brilliant and startling moonrise over the red sandstone pillars of Aultdearg, and felt the first rays of the morning sun dispel the dew. For that summer night I shared the river with its denizens undisturbed by civilisation.

By contrast, on another evening expedition the river showed another facet of her character. The day had been cold and wet, a chill breeze blowing upstream off the North Sea to Lower Aultdearg, and the hills were shrouded in mist under blue-grey clouds. Good omens were not to be found: the water was creeping up the stones (and on the Spey rising water is considered a bad sign). However, I was keen and the grilse were running. Grilse are young salmon returning to the river for the first time after gorging themselves in the sea—splendid, graceful fighters. For some hours I offered Stoat's Tails, Jeannies, Dunkelds and some home-made creations, but these were ignored. In fading light and hope well nigh lost, I moved to the tail of the pool and put a Greenwell's glory on my cast to try for sea-trout. The effect astonished me: for half an hour I had exhilarating sport. The grilse were lying in the shallows very close to the beach. Even in the gloaming I could see them, excited I think by the rising water, pursue my fly to within three feet of the stony beach, sometimes turn back abruptly into deeper water or sometimes make a last desperate lunge to drown my fly. The fact that I returned home with only one grilse is testimony to my over-enthusiasm and lack of skill, for I should by

rights have caught several. I tell this tale to indicate how unpredictable the Spey and the fish can be. But that is the essential attraction, the challenge, of angling.

Large runs of salmon and sea trout occur in the Spey. They can be spectacular, especially in late June and July when the grilse invade the river. These streamlined creatures, weighing between 4 and 9 lb, travel into fresh water, prompted by an intense migratory urge to reach the spawning redds. Their drive is so powerful that they will swim upstream even whilst the river is at very low summer levels, virtually splashing over wet stones to gain the next pool. They rest in the well-oxygenated, tumbling waters at the throats of the pools and in rocky lies. The thrill of hooking and playing a grilse full of fight in fast water has to be experienced to be appreciated. These young fish have soft mouths, incredible agility and strength, so that the outcome of every fray is in doubt until the fish is on the bank, or (as often happens) swims to freedom.

Spring runs of salmon include some very large fish. Every year several of forty pounds and over are recorded, not only in the main river but also in such tributaries as the River Avon. However, these are exceptional by any standard. The normal range for the Spey spring catch is from 12 to 20 lb, and 10 to 14 lb for the summer and autumn salmon. That is only part of the story, for in late autumn, and even after the season ends in September, some enormous fish are to be seen entering the pools in the lower reaches. These late salmon appear immune to the anglers' wiles. Nonetheless, the lower beats in late autumn are enlivened by a steady influx of fresh fish in beautiful condition who penetrate only a few miles up river.

Of recent years the evidence has become clear that the number of salmon in the spring run is decreasing and the numbers in the summer and autumn runs growing. This is supported by the observations of the ghillies in the lower and upper beats. Could this be the result of natural selection stimulated by the February to August netting season and the recent epidemics of ulcerative dermal necrosis which have affected the Spey, in common with every other salmon river in Scotland? Who knows? Perhaps a degree of ignorance is no bad thing if it means that some of the mystery of game fishing is left and if it prevents exploitation by commercial fisheries which could endanger the species.

Any account of game fishing on the Spey would be incomplete without some mention of finnock fishing. (Finnock are young sea trout.) In springtime and late summer the shoals congregate at the river mouth at Tugnet and in the lower pools. These "silver darlings" weigh about $\frac{1}{2}$ to $1\frac{1}{4}$ lb and make wonderful sport on light fly tackle. I use a 10-foot, single-handed, cane trout rod and a cast of "wee flees"—Greenwell's Glory, Peter Ross, Black Spiders and the like. The sheer variety of fishing available in the Spey is one of its outstanding attractions. As a boy, my introduction to angling was fishing for finnock. These little beauties rise greedily to a wet fly and fight spectacularly. Salty air and beating of sea against shingle at Spey Bay add an extra dimension to the charms of this river.

Characters abound along its shores, the company of ghillies adding greatly to the enjoyment of any expedition. These men are real professionals, who through many seasons have seen the pools change and develop. Advice from an experienced ghillie is of value, whether it be exhortation at a day's beginning or consolation over a dram at a bad day's end. Listening to these worthies one has to believe their accounts of days when so and so took seventeen fish before lunch, but it must be admitted that such catches are rarer today. Halcyon days may yet return, and indeed we should not be anglers if we did not believe in a second golden age. Meantime we must regale ourselves with stories like the tale of the village policeman, who fished the Fochabers water using a piece of orange peel, and regularly caught salmon!

The Laird of Pitgaveny, on whom John Buchan based his character of John McNab, was a big game hunter and sportsman of well-earned repute. On his visits to the Spey, Pitgaveny's tackle appears to have been quite extraordinary. He usually wore the kilt and spurned the use of waders. He cast a line skilfully with a long, greenheart, spliced rod held together by coarse twine. A practical gentleman if ever there was one, he used whatever materials came to hand. It is well known that a tuft from a redheaded ghillie's head, tied to a bare hook, caught salmon for the Lairdie. Such stories are apochryphal for any river of the size and reputation of the Spey, but clearly they suggest that salmon were more plentiful and co-operative in days' of yore.

However, if one needs consolation for a blank day's fishing, the countryside around the river and its animal and bird population give ample solace. At the end of an unsuccessful day's fishing I have been encouraged by many glimpses of nature caught unawares such as two buck roe deer settling their differences. This incident occurred one summer evening. A young buck swam across the river from the red sandstone cliffs at the tail of the Rock Pool. He shook himself like a wet puppy, stalked delicately across the boulders and moved quietly into the trees. A few minutes later, to the accompaniment of strident barking, he bounded back into the river, hotly pursued by a bigger buck. He crossed the river much faster than previously and closed the encounter by a tactical retreat. So engrossed were these deer in their own affairs that my presence, up to my thighs in water and rod in hand, went completely unnoticed. So an empty salmon bass is not altogether disastrous, when consolation is so readily offered by the river's fauna.

These thoughts are mainly of the river in a benign, indulgent mood. It is only human to suppress less pleasant memories, but one must always respect the power of the great Spey. A water line left in 1970 on a bothy wall nearly twenty feet above the river level at the Red Craig demonstrates the untamed forces latent in it. The Great Floods of 1829 stand as a highlight of recent history in the Spey valley.

Tales of the dreadful damage wrought at that time by the river serve as reminders that the Spey has a will of its own. Perhaps it is its savage power and unpredictability that form the quintessence of its attraction. Every season, from the bright, clear February mornings to the richly tinted autumn evenings, brings renewed yet unexpected pleasures.

Winter months are spent in preparation for next season (fly tying, tackle repairs) and in fond recollection of last season's expeditions. Surely the Spey is the only river that provides the 'Compleat Angler' with compleat angling?

A short survey of a very wide subject can do little more than point out some landmarks, well known and less well known, and if your own favourite author or work has not been included, please forgive us.

Some great Scottish literature, particularly poetry is locked away from most readers in a foreign language. Even among Scots, only a minority now understands Gaelic, although its literature is still alive and in use after fifteen centuries. It is a language with an extensive and expressive vocabulary, rich in musical words.

In the 18th century, in Britain and in Europe, an extraordinary sensation was caused by the publication of the so-called translations into English from the early Gaelic poet

Poets and Writers/Joan Rees

Ossian by James Macpherson (1736-96). These were shown up to be largely fakes, or at least masterly pieces of editing, but there is no doubt that many such epic sagas had existed and were recited to generations of audiences, sometimes accompanied by the harp, by the Highland bards. There is evidence of this, quite independent of the dubious Macpherson. Not only the chiefs, but all their people enjoyed these gatherings, and many Highland villages had their special ceilidh house. Famous latter day Gaelic poets include Alexander Macdonald and William Ross in the 18th century; Ewen Maclachlan and William Livingstone in the 19th, and George Campbell Hay and Sorley Maclean in our own century.

Scholars apart, few foreigners are tempted to learn Gaelic, but at first sight Scots itself, as Burns and earlier poets wrote it, is hard to follow. Now usually known as "Lallans", it is a Northern form of old English, with a good deal of borrowing from the French, and even Scots who know the words when spoken may well be surprised by their odd appearance on the printed page. Like the speech of many Scottish people, Lallans is so racy and expressive, with such powers of humour and pathos, that it is well worth while making the effort to understand it.

Like most Scottish poets of the 18th century and later, Burns could write in what was called 'polite' English, or in his native Lallans, as he chose. The earlier writers who could not are more difficult: but then so are Chaucer and other contemporary English writers.

In the Middle Ages, the creators of poetry were known as the Makars (makers), and the earliest of their great poems to survive was *The Bruce* by John Barbour, who lived through most of the 14th century. It is a stirring record of the Scottish struggle for independent nationality, written with simplicity, vigour, humour, and honesty, which was to have a profound effect on Walter Scott. A similar tale is told in the long work, which has been described as a verse novel, with the resounding title, *The Actes and Deidis of the Illuster and Vailyeand Campioun, Schir William Wallace, Knicht of Ellerslie*, composed or compiled by the bard known as Blind Harry.

A work in a very different vein was *The King is Quair*, believed to have been written by the first King James of Scotland. This is a love poem in the French courtly style, much influenced by Chaucer, whose works the King would have read or heard during his long exile in the English court.

Also influenced by Chaucer was one of the greatest of the Scottish medieval poets, Robert Henryson, who was writing during the second half of the 14th century, and was a schoolmaster at Dunfermline Abbey. Among his many works, perhaps the most attractive are his animal stories, based on the fables of Aesop, such as the Town Mouse and the Country Mouse; the Wolf, the Fox and the Hawker; and Chanticleer and the Fox. Here is one of Chanticleer's poor wives bewailing her sad fate after her husband's disappearance, a quotation which can also serve as an example of the language in which these poems were written (Anglicized versions are given for the benefit of non-Scottish readers):

"Quha sall our lemman be?
                quha sall us leid?
Quhen we are sad, quha sall
                unto us sing?
With his sweit bill he walk brek us
                the breid
In all this warld wes thair ane
                kynder thing?"

"Who shall our husband be?
                who shall us lead?
When we are sad, who shall
                then to us sing?
With his sweet bill he would
                break up our bread
In all this world was there a
                kinder thing?"

Writing at the same time as Henryson was the strikingly different William Dunbar, who was born in Lothian about 1460. He graduated at St Andrews University, visited Oxford and Paris, and became a priest — apparently without too much sense of vocation — attached to the court of James IV. He was one of the embassy to England which arranged the marriage of the King and Margaret Tudor, the sister of Henry VIII, and celebrated the royal marriage in a poem, *The Thrissil and the Rois* (The Thistle and the Rose). Apart from this, which earned him a small pension, he does not seem to have been a very successful courtier, and there is a certain amount of grumbling in his work about what he regarded as shabby treatment. Dunbar's poetry is extremely individual and varied, technically skilful, and presents a vivid picture of his times. Among the more famous of his productions are *The Twa Merrit Wemen and the Wedo* (The Two Married Women and the Widow), *The Flyting*, or literary quarrel which took place between Dunbar and another less well-known poet, Walter Kennedy, and probably most pleasing to the present day reader his *Lament for the Makaris*, with its haunting Latin refrain, in which he regrets all the poets who have died before him, and fears the inevitability of his own death:

Sen he has all my brether tane	*Since he has all my brothers taken*
He will nocht lat me lif alane;	*He will not let me live alone*
On forse I man his nixt pray be,	*Surely I must his next prey be*
Timor mortis conturbat me.	*The fear of death disturbeth me.*

Two other notable poets of this period were Gavin Douglas, *The Palice of Honour*, etc., and Sir David Lindsay, whose verse play, *Pleasant Satyre* is the only surviving example of the old Scottish drama.

Not so much fine verse was produced in the sixteenth century. But the works of Alexander Scott, Alexander Montgomerie and Sir Richard Maitland should be noted, and the great Ben Jonson thought so much of the poet-recluse William Drummond of Hawthornden that he walked from London to Scotland to see him. There was much interest at this time in Latin verse, of which the tutor to James VI, George Buchanan, was a leading writer; the King himself enjoyed trying his hand at poetry, and his *Basilikon Doron*, which gave advice to his son on the rules of government, on his accession to the English throne, became something of a bestseller. James also wrote about witches (he was a fearful and violent persecutor of these poor old women) and the dangers of "the vile custome of Tabacco taking."

Another writer of angry prose, who was an even more rivetting speaker, was the Calvinist leader John Knox, who wrote *The History of the Reformation*, and whose pamphlet *The First Blast of the Trumpet against the Monstrous Regiment of Women* is still well known, at least by its title, and widely misunderstood. He was not trumpeting against a contemporary version of a women's army corps, or even women in general, but against the rule and government of Queens. He had in mind principally Scotland's Queen Mary with her Roman Catholic views and supporters, and with the advent of the powerful Protestant Elizabeth I in England, no further blasts were heard of this particular trumpet. But although he kept silent, his views stayed the same. As far as he was concerned, men were ordained by God to rule over women, and any reversal of this law was "monstrous"—or against nature.

In the 16th and 17th centuries, the traditional ballads continued to be recited, added to and enjoyed, but the Reformation and Puritanism had the effect of curbing much popular literature, or converting it to serve the ends of religious propaganda. In view of the broad character of the typical Scottish sense of humour, perhaps this was understandable. Instead, came another influence, the splendid language and narrative force of the English and the Scottish Bible.

These were times of change, unrest, and for many parts of the country, misery, culminating in the controversial political Union with England in 1707. Gradually during the succeeding 18th century, when Scotland was suffering from all the effects of the last great uprising in support of Prince Charlie, men's minds began turning away from contention and violence to learning and literature Politics were no longer so important as medicine, philosophy, and the law, and instead of a parliamentary centre, Edinburgh became the cultural capital of Scotland. The University was expanding, and there arose numerous clubs and societies, devoted to a diversity of subjects.

Some writers felt the need to compete on equal terms with their English fellow authors, and deliberately set out to imitate their accents and often to improve on their prose styles. Among these were the philosopher and historian, David Hume (1711-76), Whose *Enquiry Concerning Human Understanding* and *Political Discourses* made him a European figure, and whose *History of Great Britain* proved a major influence for many years. His friend, Adam Smith of Glasgow University (1723-90) revolutionized current ideas about economics with *The Wealth of Nations.* Tobias Smollett (1721-71) succeeded so brilliantly with his novels that he is usually named in that great 18th century quartet which also includes Richardson, Fielding, and Sterne. James Thomson (1700-48) with his *Seasons* was among the band of poets who led the way from the classical Augustans to the Romantics. With the *Man of Feeling*, Henry Mackenzie (1745-1831) produced one of the most popular of the fashionable novels of sensibility. While James Boswell (1740-95) with his *Life of Samuel Johnson,* not only wrote the life of one of the most famous Englishmen of his generation, but produced so fine and famous a biography that for most people now it tends to overshadow the great Doctor's own productions. Not only this, but by taking the Doctor to the Hebrides and writing about it, Boswell did a great deal to open up the beauties of the country and encourage the tourism from the South that was then just beginning. When he wrote in his *Journal* of this tour, "To see Mr Samuel Johnson lying in Prince Charlie's bed, in the Isle of Skye, in the house of Flora Macdonald, struck me with such a group of ideas as it is not easy for words to describe as the mind perceives them," we can well believe him.

At the same time as many turned their eyes to England, another important group, anxious perhaps to assert their national pride, began digging into the treasure-trove of the old songs and ballads of Scotland, and realising anew the special resources and powers of their native language. The first of such anthologies to appear early in the 18th century was James Watson's *Choice Collection of Scottish Poems*; But the most energetic and important figure in this revival was Allan Ramsay (1685-1758) who began life as a successful wigmaker, but whose great love of poetry and conviviality caused him to change course and become an equally successful bookseller, collector, and writer of verse, the recognised "laureate of the streets." He has sometimes been criticized for trying to improve the works he was collecting, but he preserved more than he spoiled. Best known of his rescue operations are *Christis Kirk, Scots Songs, Evergreen,* and *The Tea Table Miscellany.* The most popular of his original pieces was *The Gentle Shepherd.*

The songs and ballads had an immediate popular success, and helped to inspire the best work of the brilliant, erratic Robert Fergusson (1750-74), who unfortunately was to die so young. His poem *The Daft Days* describing the celebrations for the passing of the old and the seeing-in of the new year, was a serious original work deliberately written with the added force of the Scots words.

Now mirk December's dowie face	*Now dark December's saddened face,*
Glours our the rigs wi' sour grimace,	*Stares o'er the hills with sour grimace,*
While, thro' his minimum of space,	*While, through his minimum of space*
The bleer-ey'd sun,	*The dim-eyed sun,*
Wi' blinkin light and stealing pace,	*With blinking light and stealing pace,*
His race doth run.	*His race doth run.*

Fergusson followed this with other major poems: *The King's Birthday in Edinburgh; Geordie and Davie; The Rising of the Session* and *The Sitting of the Session*, and in *Auld Reekie* (Old Smoky), he recorded a true impression of the Edinburgh he knew so well. It is no exaggeration to say that Fergusson prepared the way for the most famous and best loved of all Scottish poets, Robert Burns.

The life of Burns (1759-96) is well known in general terms—the poor farm boy; the writer fashionably lionised as the "ploughman poet"; the professional exciseman who was constantly hard up; the playboy, helplessly fond of women, hoping, moping, drinking, sinking, singing like a scandalous angel until he died in his thirties. He had arresting good looks, star quality, dramatic appeal, and a genius for narrative and lyric poetry. *Tam o'Shanter, Auld Lang Syne* (Old Long Ago), and many other familiar favourites, perhaps not so well known as we like to think, all make rewarding rereading.

Visitors to Scotland have long sought out Burns's birthplace at Alloway, the Auld Brig o'
Doon, and the house where he died at Dumfries.

Robert Burns is loved in Scotland because of his faults, while Sir Walter Scott is
admired for his virtues. As Burns was fired by the old Scottish songs, so Scott was
inspired by the Ballads, in particular those of the Border country, the lands of the Tweed
and the Yarrow, which he has made so much his own. Walter Scott (1771-1832), who was
a successful lawyer and Sheriff of Selkirk, began his literary career as a poet and
achieved fame and popularity with his *Border Minstrelsy, The Lay of the Last Minstrel,
Marmion,* and *The Lady of the Lake.* It was not until 1814 that he anonymously
published *Waverley,* the first of the series of novels that until he revealed his identity
made him famous as the Great Unknown. The effect of Scott's novels on the literature of
Scotland can hardly be over-estimated, and he was also the first serious writer of the now

familiar historical novel. The tragedy of his life was the bankruptcy of the publishing company with which he was associated and his Herculean efforts to pay off his debts by his writing, and to keep the beautiful house of Abbotsford, which was not only his home, but the realisation of a dream. He managed to do both, but at the expense of his health. Even for those who no longer read his novels, his courageous struggle, the integrity of his character, much of which is modestly revealed by his *Journals,* remain an inspiring example.

In the third volume of the second edition of Scott's Border Minstrelsy were some ballads which had been given to him by James Hogg (1770-1835), the humble but gifted poet who became known as the Ettrick Shepherd, and also wrote a remarkable novel, *The Private Memories and Confessions of a Justified Sinner.* Another interesting novelist of this time is John Galt (1779-1839) whose *Annals of the Parish* draws a careful picture of everyday country life.

An aspect of the 19th century Scottish literary scene which should not be forgotten is the establishment of the critical reviews, such as *Blackwood's* and the *Edinburgh* which, both for good and bad, wielded such influential power.

Robert Louis Stevenson was born in Edinburgh in 1850, and died far away in Samoa, where he had settled in his lifelong search for health, forty-four years later. The many wearisome days he was forced to spend in bed as a child played an important part in the development of his imagination, and in his later ability to communicate with young people and enchant them with his writing. As his wife was to note, every poem in his *A Child's Garden of Verses* "was a bit of his own childhood." *Treasure Island, Kidnapped,*

and *The Bottle Imp*, and *Dr. Jekyll and Mr. Hyde* are outstanding examples of brilliant short stories which are also allegorical fantasies.

Novelist, essayist, travel writer, and poet, both in English and Scots, honoured in the South Sea Islands with the title of Tusitala, the teller of tales, he died at work on what was likely to have proved his masterpiece, *Weir of Hermiston*. He always gained immense satisfaction from his writing: "The direct return, the wages of the trade, are small, but the indirect wages of the life are incalculably great. No other business offers a man his daily bread upon such joyful terms."

Stevenson was well aware of the special strength to be gained by writing in his native Scots, and much vigorous verse was being produced during these years, as can be seen in the excellent volume of *Scottish Verse, 1851-1951*, edited by Douglas Young. With writers at work such as John Davidson, James Logie Robertson, Andrew Lang, James

Thomson, the weaver poet of the broadsheets, William McGonagall, and many others, it is clear that what is known as the Scottish Renaissance had been for a long while gradually gathering steam. Undoubtedly the most famous and influential writer in the movement has been C. M. Grieve, better known as Hugh MacDiarmid. Although his political beliefs have made him a controversial figure, there can be no doubt of his quality as a poet, both in Lallans and in English. His best known poem is *A Drunk Man Looks at a Thistle*, but he has produced a large body of challenging work, and has been acclaimed the greatest Scottish poet since Dunbar.

In the past, no doubt because of the long period of puritan disapproval, few Scottish writers were drawn to the theatre. But the 20th century has seen a re-awakening of interest in the drama. Known first for his reminiscences of his old home at Kirriemuir and Edinburgh, *A Window in Thrums, The Little Minister, An Edinburgh Eleven*, Sir James Barrie (1860-1937) became one of the outstanding playwrights of his day, and audiences were moved and intrigued by that strange tale of the islands, *Mary Rose*, and the Celtic sense of a fantastic world beyond reality with which much of his work is embued. James Bridie (1888-1951) was another successful dramatist, whose best known play, *The Anatomist*, was based on the Edinburgh scandal caused by the murderous activities of Burke and Hare. Today, with the wider and more appreciative audiences created by television, and the challenge of the Edinburgh Festival, many talented Scottish writers are beginning to bring their skills to the writing of plays.   Our own century has produced many extremely successful Scottish novelists, whose works have been enjoyed by millions at home and abroad. Sir Compton Mackenzie was writing entertaining works of tremendous variety throughout his long life, and will be remembered as a broadcaster and Scottish personality. The film of his *Whisky Galore* amused audiences all over the world.

John Buchan, Eric Linklater, A. J. Cronin, Josephine Tey (Gordon Daviot), J. I. M. Stewart (Michael Innes), Muriel Spark, and Alastair MacLean form an impressive list of best sellers. Of exceptional interest are George Douglas Brown, *The House with Green Shutters;* John MacDougal Hay, *Gillespie;* David Lindsay, *Voyage to Arcturus;* Lewis Grassic Gibbon, *A Scots Quair*, and Neil Gunn, *The Silver Darlings.*

Most of all by the Scots themselves, there have been certain criticisms. There has been disapproval of what has been known as the "Kailyaird school" with its outlook of smug narrow provincialism; too much pawky humour; and an excess of sentimentality. But the best of Scottish writing has a tough individuality, a terseness and vigour, a realistic humour, a sense of history, a Celtic other-worldly awareness, a great gift for story telling, and a sensitive handling of description, character, and language. The intertwining of so many strands of tradition, the Gaelic, the Scots, the English, the French Romance, the intimate knowledge of the bible, has produced a richness of texture and colour, as in the Tartans and the tweeds. Above all, there is the prevailing sense of the country itself, in all its different scenes, aspects, and weathers; the bracing atmosphere of the heather scented moors, the pure air of the pine clad mountains, and the fresh winds from the far northern seas.

In December 1804 a number of gentlemen of Argyll employed a Writer to the Signet (that unique Scottish brand of lawyer) to draw up a petition. A distance of no more than 25 miles as the crow flies, their petition pointed out to the government, separated two of their most important towns: Rothesay, centre of the growing herring industry and Inveraray, commercial, legal and administrative centre for the area. Yet the distance by road, they declared, was no less than 117 miles.

   They wanted a new road, and some government financial aid to help provide it. They were not alone in their petition. In many other parts of Scotland people at that time,

around the end of the 18th and the beginning of the 19th century, were realising that survival meant roads. Times were changing and old economic systems breaking up. Now the Highlands must get its beef, wool and mutton to Central and Lowland Scotland where the Industrial Revolution was creating population centres in the new Scotland of shipyards, mine and factory, which must in turn find swift routes for its products to the lucrative markets of England and the ports which fed the Empire.

Nowhere in Britain was the prospect a more daunting one. Mountainous terrain and the deep arms of sea lochs and firths penetrating the country conspired to make the shortest distance between two points on the map into a formidable journey over the ground.

As a nation Scotland had to tame its landscape or wither. As it turned out this was one of those turning points of history when the moment produced the men. In the course of no more than three decades Scotland gave birth to some of the greatest engineers the world has known, men like Watt, McAdam, Telford and Rennie. They were mostly men of humble origin who not only met the challenge of the times at home but went on to leave enduring monuments beyond their native country. After roads came canals, railways, bridges, steamships—and in every new venture Scotland's engineers were to be found pioneering the way.

It has to be admitted that the start of Scotland's road programme came from an Englishman. General Wade, sent by King George to subdue the unruly northern province after the 1715 Jacobite Rising, opened a few shrewd Highland eyes to the benefits when he built 250 miles of road round his military stations at Fort William and Fort Augustus to facilitate the quick movement of troops.

"Had you seen the roads before they were made
You would lift up your hands and bless General Wade"
said a couplet at the time.

However, having taken the point, the resourceful Scots needed no further lessons from South of the border. In a few years it was Scotsmen who were in demand to improve the roads of London.

First of these was John Loudon McAdam, born at Ayr in 1756, a member of the long outlawed McGregor clan, the use of whose very name was proscribed by law.

It was McAdam who worked out that roads needed to be built with small broken stones, angular in shape, compacted, cambered and drained. When English counties saw what he had done for his native Ayrshire they were soon clamouring for his services and people talked of "Macadamising" the roads. In his dedication to his job of road building he travelled 30,000 miles and spent £5,000 of his own money (you would have to multiply that about 20 times to get some idea of today's value), but in the end a grateful Parliament in Whitehall voted him £10,000 for his services. The word "tarmac" still commemorates his name.

Born only two years later, the son of a shepherd in Eskdale, Dumfriesshire, was Thomas Telford. Largely self-educated and early left fatherless he began working life as a village mason and when he died was buried in Westminster Abbey, fittingly recognised as one of the greatest engineers of all time. Even today you cannot travel about the British Isles without being constantly reminded of him, by such feats as the London to Holyhead road, now known as the A5, with its great bridge across the Menai Straits, the Ellesmere canal with the remarkable Pont Cyssylte viaduct spanning 1,000 feet of the Dee valley, the first ever iron bridge at Coalbrookdale and so on.

In his 77 years Telford fitted in enough work for several ordinary lifetimes, leaving behind him over 1,000 miles of new roads, 1,200 bridges, 43 harbours and several canals, including the Caledonian.

One writer has declared that Telford was a man who advanced his country by at least a century. Another biographer wrote: "From being one of the idlest and most backward countries in Europe, Scotland became rapidly one of the most progressive and began to exercise an influence on literature, science and industry out of all proportion to its population. That this opportunity of development was brought about largely through

the achievements of civil engineering enterprise was perhaps no great surprise to Telford. He was a far-seeing and shrewd observer and he knew the latent qualities of his own countrymen."

Perhaps Telford's greatest extant memorial in Scotland is the Caledonian Canal, linking the North Sea with the Atlantic by a 60 mile route from Inverness to Fort William down the Great Glen. Seamen today bless it just as much as their predecessors did when it opened 150 years ago, for it saves a voyage of nearly 200 miles round an inhospitable coast, including the treacherous tides of the Pentland Firth and the stormy seas off Cape Wrath.

Though lionised in London, where hundreds visited his coffee house lodgings in the hope of hearing "Laughing Tom" discoursing on engineering, Telford never forgot his poor beginnings and placed great stress on the social value of his schemes.

His pride in the engineering achievement of the Caledonian Canal, which would take a 32-gun man o'war through the heart of the Highlands as easily as a fishing boat, was well matched by his missionary zeal for the scheme on the grounds that it would "furnish employment for the industrious and valuable part of the people in their own country" This the Caledonian Canal did, keeping some 900 labourers occupied for nearly 20 years at a time when emigration or destitution were the only choices facing thousands of Highland families being evicted from their traditional tenant holdings to make way for sheep farms.

Telford was also concerned during the same period with the improvement of Scotland's other notable canal, the Crinan. This cuts the Mull of Kintyre and, as John Knox said, "brings the people of the Highlands nearer to Glasgow and the seats of trade and commerce by more than 100 miles every voyage."

The Crinan Canal was originally constructed by another great Scottish engineer, John Rennie, a contemporary of Telford's whose achievements were almost as great, but who has been rather over-shadowed in the history books by 'Laughing Tom'.

Rennie was born of East Lothian yeoman farmer stock in 1761. By the time he was 19 he had a thriving business building and equipping flour mills, but in 1783 pocketed his savings and rode south on horseback, where he soon made a new reputation. Like Telford he too has left his mark all over Britain. Southwark Bridge, the old London Bridge, the old Waterloo Bridge, the East India docks, Plymouth breakwater and the Kennet and Avon canal which linked the Thames to the Severn are just a few of his great works.

Rennie was a modest man who declined a knighthood offered to him by the Prince Regent and he never failed to remember the humble folk he came from. On one occasion he was travelling by stage coach to stay with the Earl of Eglington at Ardrossan Castle. As the coach was crossing a lonely moor without a habitation in sight, an axle broke. Their upper class fellow passengers were helpless, so Rennie and an engineering colleague dismantled the broken member and walked with it several miles to the nearest smithy. The smith, however, pleaded the repair was too difficult for him and would have to be sent to Ayr, which would leave the coach and passengers benighted on the moor. At this point Rennie slipped into his native brogue, and talked 'shop', taking off his jacket ready for action. The smith, recognising now a fellow craftsman. and seeing he would have expert help instead of a heavy single-handed job, set to work with a will, with the famous engineer acting as striker. Soon Rennie was on his way back to the coach to assemble the repaired axle. However the rather superior passengers, far from being grateful to the men who had saved them from a cold and uncomfortable night on the open moor, now thought it disgraceful that a pair who were obviously grubby artisans should have presumed to travel as inside passengers with their betters, instead of on top as was the usual lot of poor folk, and declined to speak with them for the rest of the journey.

But the last laugh was with Rennie. A few days later some of the same travellers paid an obsequious call on the Earl only to find with him the common coach repairer, an honoured guest at the Castle.

These early pioneering engineers were less specialised than those of today and men like Rennie were as accomplished at mechanical engineering as they were at construction work, which in their day had just come to be dubbed 'civil engineering.' Rennie in fact spent part of his career working for that great Scots genius of mechanical engineering James Watt.

Watt is perhaps better known than he strictly deserves compared with some of his contemporaries, largely because of the legend of his being scolded as a boy for idly watching the kettle lid rise and fall as the water boiled, dreaming of how the steam's energy might be harnessed. This ranks with Alfred and the cakes and Bruce and the spider among the stories every schoolboy knows.

Watt was born in Greenock in 1736 and began work as an instrument maker in Glasgow. When someone sent him an engine made by the great English engineer Newcomen to repair, he saw ways to improve it and so began to build the first steam engines with two stroke reciprocating action, which were far more practical and economical. These enabled much more progress to be made with pumping work for the developing coal mines and booming canals.

Watt might have become the first great railway pioneer, especially after he employed another mechanical genius from Ayrshire, William Murdock, who had discovered how to use burning coal gas effectively to power steam engines. Murdock built a small moving steam engine which eye witnesses said "went like a little demon," but Watt, immersed in the immediate problems of stationary steam power, discouraged him and said that "engines that move about are but an idle dream." It was left to the Englishman George Stephenson to become the father of the railway.

However when the historic Rocket puffed its way down the lines from Stockton to Darlington Scottish engineers were not slow to realise the implications and the country was soon as much in the grip of railway mania as the rest of Britain. Early railways were nothing if not cut-throat competitive private enterprise, and in Scotland a battle royal was waged between two great rivals, The Caledonian Railway operating from Glasgow and the North British running out of Edinburgh.

As ever in Scotland, natural geography was a dominant factor, especially the huge estuaries or firths, which caused long detours. The company which could shorten its routes would win the battle for profitable traffic.

In 1849 the newly appointed manager and engineer of the Edinburgh line Thomas Bouch tried to persuade the shareholders to let him build bridges over the Forth and Tay to shorten the route to Perth and Dundee. Such a feat was thought to be impossible, so the bridge plans were pigeon-holed and Bouch brought forth a new scheme which was given the go-ahead. By 1851 he had designed and put into operation a 'floating railway' of steam ferries across both rivers, the first of their kind in the world.

For the Forth crossing Bouch had built by Robert Napier of Glasgow a paddle steamer called the *Leviathan*, 172 ft long and 54 ft beam, wide enough to take three lines of railway wagons. The wagons were shunted at the riverside on to an inclined plane which was hauled up or down according to the state of the tide, to transfer the rolling stock to and from the vessel. In this fashion 34 wagons at a time were loaded in just over five minutes for a crossing which took 26 minutes.

The system was not superseded until the opening of the Forth railway bridge in 1890, the *Leviathan* making four or five double trips a day and carrying 75,000 wagons in a year. A smaller vessel, the *Napier*, provided a similar service across the Tay, and the two ferries captured for the North British a large share of their competitor's traffic, especially the profitable coal from the Fifeshire pits.

Still Bouch dreamed of a bridge and eventually gained support for his scheme to span the river Tay. His bridge was opened on the last day of May 1878 and North British shares soared in anticipation. After the royal train had passed over the bridge en route from Balmoral, Queen Victoria summoned Mr Bouch to Windsor and sent him home Sir Thomas Bouch.

Alas, the glory was soon shattered. The following year on December 28th came the great Tay Bridge disaster when a hurricane toppled all 13 of the bridge's high girders and 12 of its cast iron piers into the river, carrying with them a whole train with 75 men, women and children, who were all drowned.

A public enquiry found that Sir Thomas Bouch had failed to make proper calculation

for wind force when designing the bridge. He died within a year of a broken heart and his plans for a structure across the Clyde, greater than any other bridge work attempted in Britain at that time, were placed in other hands. Happily what emerged was one of the handsomest and most famous bridges in the world.

It incidentally gave the English language a new saying, "like the Forth Bridge," arising from the fact that when maintenance men have finished painting the 54,160 tons of steel and 6,500,000 rivets which make up its 135 acres of surface area, it is time to start again! Now in the motorway age the famous Forth railway bridge has a road bridge for an equally handsome sister.

While these tremendous improvements in land communications were going on the Scots were also turning their engineering prowess to the improvement of travel by sea. As early as 1787 an inventive laird called Patrick Miller of Dalswinton built a mechanical ship propelled by man-power in the shape of 30 men working at a capstan which turned a paddle wheel. He is said to have crossed the North Sea with it at an average four knots and to have presented it to the King of Sweden, which may have accounted for the fact that the idea did not receive much encouragement from Whitehall. A few years later he teamed up with a poor miner called Symington from Wanlockhead who had designed and built his own steam engine. Together they built a paddle steamer which travelled along the Forth-Clyde canal at six knots before an astonished audience of notables including Robert Burns. Unfortunately most of them dismissed it as an amusing novelty.

One more perceptive spectator was William Bell, a millright who had worked under Rennie. After many frustrations Bell built the first successful paddle steam vessel, the *Comet,* and launched her at Helensburgh on the Clyde in 1812. Two years later on the Clyde, William Denny built the *Marjorie,* which became the first steamer to cross the English Channel. They were the pioneers of the great Scottish shipyards which eventually built some of the greatest ships in the world, including all three Queens and most of the other great Cunarders.

At the same time other Scots engineers were trying to make the sea coast safer for shipping, the most notable among them Robert Stevenson, engineer to the Commissioners of Northern Lights. His greatest achievement was the lighthouse on the Bell Rock, notoriously celebrated in legend and verse as a graveyard for sailors since the Middle Ages. As the rock only uncovers for a very short time at low water the task called for tremendous ingenuity and dogged determination. The 115 ft high tower, completed in four years, still stands sentinel there today.

Men like these were the giants of the golden age of Scottish engineering, but they were in a sense only the tip of the iceberg. They taught their assistants, supervisors and successors, so establishing a national tradition which is still as strong as it was in the 18th and 19th centuries. In most parts of the world today, where there is road or runway being driven, a bridge or oil rig to be built, ships' machinery or power stations to be tended, you are likely to come across an engineer called Mac.

Captions to photographs

4/A view of Southern and Central Scotland taken by the Earth Resources Technology Satellite which circles our planet every $103\frac{3}{4}$ minutes at a height of approximately 559 miles.
Picture by Aerofilms Limited

8/Britain's first integrated chemical pulp and paper mill built by Wiggins Teape produces 80000 tons of pulp and 50000 tons of paper each year. The mill is situated at Corpach in the shadow of Ben Nevis.
Picture by Wiggins Teape Limited

12/This Selkirk monument commemorates the return from Flodden Field (1513) of the sole survivor of the town's 80 strong contingent; he proudly displays the captured British Standard.

17/Remains of the 12th century Cistercian Abbey at Melrose described in Scott's Lay of the Last Minstrel. The heart of Scotland's patriot King, Robert Bruce, is buried here.

20/The wild countryside around Glencoe, the scene in the early hours of a cold winter morning in 1692 of the massacre of the Macdonalds—a story of treachery and the betrayal of hospitality.

24/Young gulls waiting to be fed. These birds are usually reared by both parents, who share the work between them. Whilst one hunts for food, the other stays at the nest to guard the young from predators, including other gulls.

30/Dramatically dominating the capital, Edinburgh Castle is an unfailing reminder of the country's long and eventful history, linking the past and its many royal associations to the new traditions of the Edinburgh Festival.
Picture by The Scottish Tourist Board

32/Originally built in 1628, Braemar Castle was destroyed at the time of the Jacobite risings and rebuilt around 1748. Queen Victoria enjoyed the traditional games and dances of the annual Braemar gathering, as do the Royal Family today.

36/The round towers and turret of Glamis Castle, ancestral home of the Queen Mother.

41/Fishing vessels in Eyemouth harbour, a busy fishing port, though not so bustling as in the herring heyday at the turn of the century. Here in 1856 the first decked drifter was built, greatly improving the lot of the Scottish fishermen.

44/Dappled sunlight on a boat's hull, the mingled smell of tarred rope and salt water are pleasures still to be enjoyed in most Scottish harbours. In many places container terminals or yacht marinas have left only childhood memories.

45/The deep bite of rope marks into the Samson post gives an indication of the strain endured by men and gear to win the sea harvest. Despite modern improvements, fishing in Scottish waters is still a hard and dangerous occupation.

48/Still-life Scottish style: a selection of some of the finest Scottish cakes and buns: scones, Scotch or black bun a traditional Hogmanay cake, Aberdeen crullas, Selkirk bannock a favourite with Queen Victoria, and rich, dark gingerbread.
Photograph by Philip Pace

52/The new road bridge spanning the Firth of Forth. This bridge, one of

Europe's longest suspension bridges with a centre span of over 1000 yards was opened to the public in 1964.
Picture by Scottish Television and Grampian Sales Limited

57/Sea Quest, situated 110 miles off the Aberdeen coast, was launched in January 1966 and has a floating weight of 7500 tons. About £12000 per day is spent on maintaining her and her support vessels.
Picture by BP

60/Part of the new extension to the passenger terminal at Glasgow's Abbotsinch Airport. The main airport building was opened to the public in 1966 by Her Majesty the Queen.

61/British Caledonian Airways' lion rampant on one of this carrier's inter-continental Boeing 707s, which carry passengers over many major routes throughout the world.

62/A Highland malt-whisky distillery on Speyside. Many such distilleries are located in the remoter areas and they depend upon the unique qualities of local water; the greatest concentration of distilleries is found in the Spey valley.
Picture by The Scotch Whisky Association.

65/Some of the most precious and purest water in the world pouring down from the granite peaks of the Highlands to join the fast-flowing and salmon-rich Spey and to play its part in distilling Scotland's most precious and purest spirit.
Picture by The Scotch Whisky Association

69/After distillation Scotch whisky is filled into oak casks and left to mature in cool, dark warehouses. The soft Scottish air slowly brings the spirit to perfection.
Picture by The Scotch Whisky Association

73/A profusion of wild flowers and grasses decorate the banks of the Spey throughout the Summer adding for the fisherman to the charms of this celebrated river.

81/Brig o'Doon, Alloway: the 13th century bridge over the River Doon made world-famous by Robert Burns in his poem, Tam o'Shanter.

82/The reflective waters of the River Doon beside which, in the humble farm cottage built by his father, Robert Burns was born on 25 January 1759.

83/Not far from Braemar Castle in this stone cottage in Castleton Terrace, Robert Louis Stevenson wrote part of Treasure Island, the adventure story which continues to enchant each succeeding generation.

84/The monument in Selkirk market place to Sir Walter Scott who started his career as a lawyer and was for many years Sheriff of Selkirk County, before achieving fame as poet and novelist.

86/The Spey-Garmouth railway bridge, now dis-used, which once carried trains from Inverness across the wide mouth of the river Spey before it flows into the Moray Firth.

89/The old Spey road bridge at Craigellachie. Now closed to traffic it is nevertheless a permanent tribute to its designer Thomas Telford.

92/The Pitlochry Dam is an example of the hydro-electric development on the river Tummel. This dam created a new loch known as Faskallay. A salmon-pass was built to enable the adult fish to make their way to the higher reaches of the river.